CONTENTS

SEVEN DAYS IN
CAPE TOWN

SEVEN DAYS IN
CAPE TOWN

Sean Fraser

Published by Struik Travel & Heritage
(an imprint of Random House Struik (Pty) Ltd)
Company Reg. No. 1966/003153/07
80 McKenzie Street, Cape Town, 8001
PO Box 1144, Cape Town, 8000, South Africa

First published in 1998, Reprinted 1999, 2000, 2001, 2002 (twice), 2004, 2005;
Second edition published in 2006, Reprinted in 2007, 2008;
Third edition published in 2010

ISBN 978 1 77007 869 7

1 3 5 7 9 10 8 6 4 2

Publisher: Claudia Dos Santos
Managing editor: Roelien Theron
Editor: Alfred LeMaitre
Designer: Sonia Hedenskog, Catherine Coetzer
Cartographers: Mark Seabrook, Desireé Oosterberg, Eloïse Moss, Genene Hart
Picture researcher: Carmen Swanepoel
Indexer: Annelene van der Merwe

Reproduced by Hirt & Carter Cape (Pty) Ltd
Printed and bound by Times International Printing

FRONT COVER *Table Mountain, seen from Bloubergstrand across Table Bay.*
BACK COVER *(Top right) Fishermen at Hout Bay harbour; (Centre right) Klein Constantia; (Bottom right) Beach cabins at Muizenberg.*
SPINE *The Disa uniflora, or Pride of Table Mountain, is the symbol of the Cape.*
HALF TITLE PAGE *The blustery winds that plague sunbathers are welcomed by kite-flyers and kite-surfers at Blouberg Beach.*
TITLE PAGES *The sun sets over Cape Town's Atlantic seaboard and the city centre skirting Table Bay beyond.*
THIS PAGE *The peninsula is draped in the gentle colours of dusk as the sun sets over False Bay.*
PAGE 6 *Table Mountain slopes towards the plush suburb of Camps Bay.*
PAGE 9 *Lion's Head and Signal Hill stand guard over the suburbs of Green Point, Sea Point and Fresnaye. The affluent suburbs of Camps Bay and Llandudno lie just beyond.*
PAGES 10–11 *At night, the Mother City – home to more than four million Capetonians – is transformed into a playground for locals and visitors alike.*

ACKNOWLEDGEMENTS

I am extremely proud that this, the first book I ever tackled as a writer rather than an editor, has enjoyed so much success in the marketplace. It would not, however, have been as well received – or as useful – had it not been for the meticulous research undertaken by my great friend Brenda Brickman, who not only worked through all my pages of notes to verify every fact, but wielded the whip to make sure that when I submitted the first draft of the first edition it was virtually word perfect. While Brenda is no longer with us, her painstaking effort and unfaltering dedication remains evident on every page in this new, fully revised edition. My thanks, too, to my wife, Tracey. I trust that the patience and endurance she showed on this project bodes well for a long and happy married life, despite the demands of a husband in publishing. This edition is dedicated to my dear friend and colleague, Brenda; to my Dad and late Mom, who encouraged the reader and writer in me; to my wife, Tracey, and sons, Darren and Aidan, who I hope will be inspired by this book, and others, to read and to write, and appreciate this remarkable city.

PHOTOGRAPHIC CREDITS

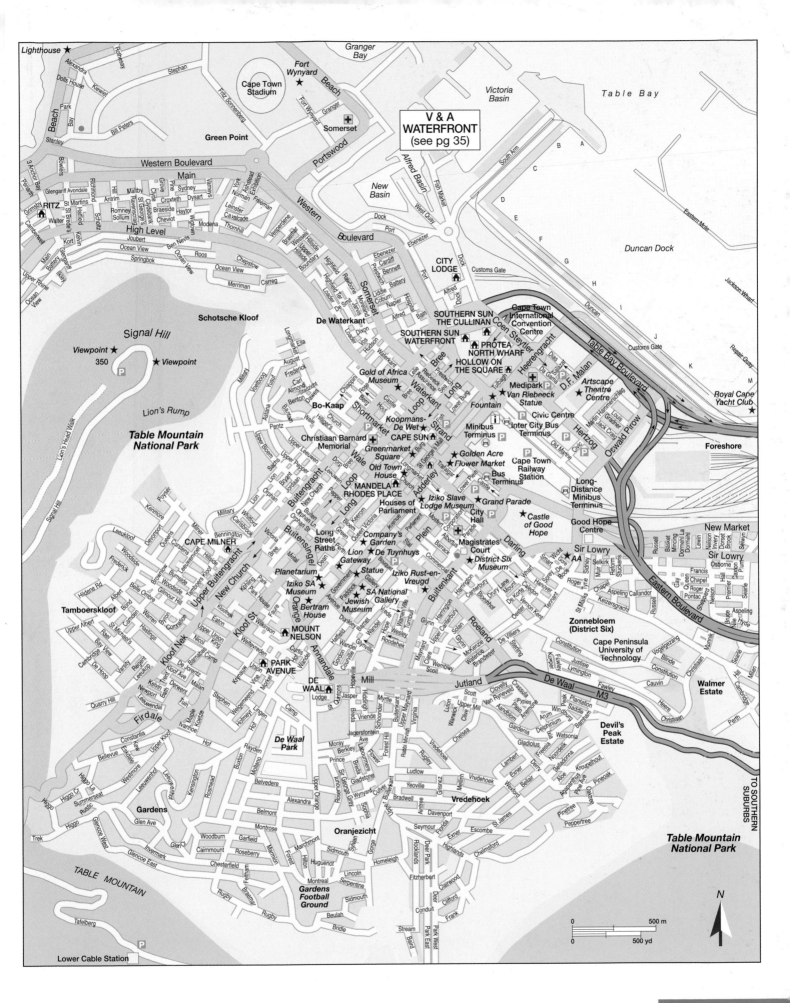

Lighthouse ★

V & A
WATERFRONT
(see pg 35)

Table Bay

Cape Town
Stadium

Fort
Wynyard ★

Granger
Bay

Victoria
Basin

Green Point

Western Boulevard

Main

High Level

New
Basin

Duncan Dock

CITY
LODGE

Customs Gate

Schotsche Kloof

De Waterkant

SOUTHERN SUN
THE CULLINAN

Cape Town
International
Convention
Centre

Signal Hill

Viewpoint ★

350 ★ Viewpoint

Bo-Kaap

Gold of Africa
Museum

SOUTHERN SUN
WATERFRONT

PROTEA
NORTH WHARF
HOLLOW ON
THE SQUARE

Medipark

Artscape
Theatre
Centre

Royal Cape
Yacht Club

Lion's Rump

Table Mountain
National Park

Koopmans-
De Wet

CAPE SUN

Van Riebeeck
Statue

Civic Centre
Inter City Bus
Terminus

Foreshore

Christiaan Barnard
Memorial

Greenmarket
Square

Old Town
House

MANDELA
RHODES PLACE

Minibus
Terminus

Fountain

Golden Acre
Flower Market

Bus
Terminus

Cape Town
Railway
Station

Long-
Distance
Minibus
Terminus

New Market

Houses of
Parliament

Iziko Slave
Lodge Museum

Grand Parade

City
Hall

Good Hope
Centre

Sir Lowry

Sir Lowry

CAPE MILNER

Long
Street
Baths

Company's
Garden

Lion
Gateway

De Tuynhuys

Magistrates'
Court

District Six
Museum

Castle
of Good
Hope

Tamboerskloof

Planetarium

Iziko SA
Museum

Statue

SA National
Gallery

Iziko Rust-en-
Vreugd

Zonnebloem
(District Six)

Bertram
House

Jewish
Museum

Cape Peninsula
University of
Technology

Walmer
Estate

MOUNT
NELSON

PARK
AVENUE

DE
WAAL
Lodge

Mill

Jutland

De Waal M3

Devil's
Peak
Estate

De Waal
Park

Gardens

Vredehoek

TO
SOUTHERN
SUBURBS

Oranjezicht

TABLE MOUNTAIN

Gardens
Football
Ground

Table Mountain
National Park

N

0   500 m
0   500 yd

Lower Cable Station

7

Introduction

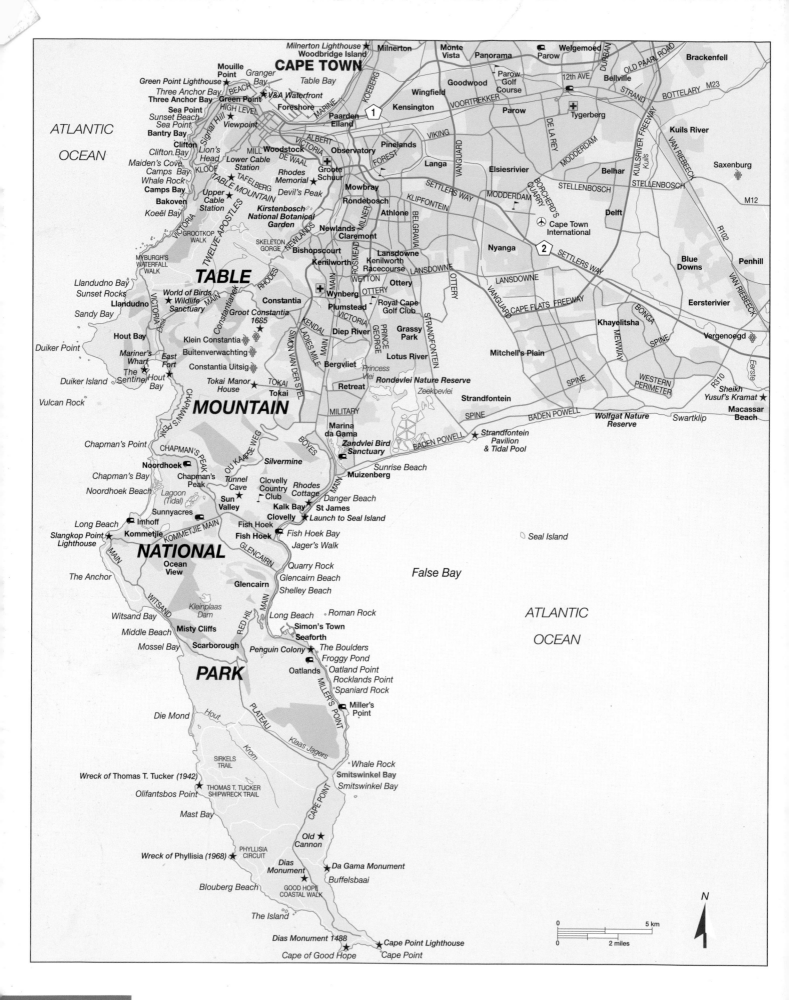

Hundreds of thousands of foreign tourists visit South Africa every year, and most of these visitors plan a stop in Cape Town, the pride of the southern African subcontinent. Blessed with blue skies, a balmy climate, a rich cultural heritage and a magnificent backdrop of ocean and mountain, the Mother City boasts a profusion of museums, art galleries, restaurants, shops, theatres, night spots and landmarks. Presided over by Table Mountain and skirted by the Atlantic Ocean and a string of exquisite beaches, top attractions include the bustling V&A Waterfront, the famed Kirstenbosch National Botanical Garden, the Table Mountain National Park, the Cape Winelands and Robben Island.

Seven Days in Cape Town offers an introduction to these special places, and to many other lesser-known sites and attractions. Seven day-tours escort you through the peninsula, covering seven different areas of the city and its immediate surrounds. In addition, the six special excursions take you to the outlying areas, without which a visit to the city is incomplete: the flowers of the West Coast, the Cape Winelands or the Whale Route. Some are best seen over a day or two and visitors may want to stay overnight – especially if the drive to your destination takes up much of your day. A number of routes are suggested, with street addresses, websites, e-mail addresses and telephone numbers for the traveller's convenience.

These scenic routes are best travelled by car – ideal for a leisurely drive and the opportunity to stop and admire the sunset or investigate the unique flora and fauna of the wondrous Cape Floral Kingdom – but areas serviced by regular bus routes have been indicated, and the Metrorail train service runs down the length of the Cape Peninsula. The Bus Rapid Transport (BRT) system of dedicated bus and taxi lanes covers the inner city and access routes to the airport and some northern suburbs. Naturally, special tours and packages may also be provided by the tourist organisations or travel agents operating within the city.

Most of the suggested tours in this book may be completed in one day, but if you're really in a hurry – and prepared to miss out on some of the many tempting attractions – it is possible to tour the entire peninsula in just a few hours.

The final pages of this book are devoted to directories that cover shopping, dining and entertainment in the Cape Town area. Also included is a calendar of events for advance planning.

Whatever the reason for your visit, and with all these options from which to choose, it's easy to fall in love with the city of Cape Town. We hope that you will take just seven days – or more, if your itinerary allows – to discover this beautiful city, its people and its culture.

Sean Fraser

DAY

1

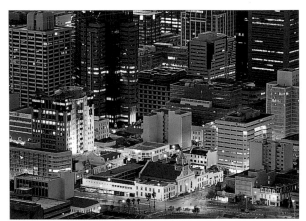

HEART OF THE
MOTHER CITY

HEART OF THE MOTHER CITY

Foreshore and Heerengracht • Adderley Street • Company's Garden • Buitenkant Street
Strand Street • De Waterkant • District Six • Greenmarket Square • Long Street

Running down the middle of what is today the city's Central Business District (CBD) is Adderley Street, the modern thoroughfare that replaced the old Heerengracht or 'Gentleman's Walk', a simple road stretching along the banks of the canal that linked the Dutch settlement to the docks on Table Bay. This conglomeration of Dutch and Victorian architecture, interspersed with modern wonders of glass and concrete, is the heart of Cape Town, and on either side of Adderley Street is an eclectic array of sightseeing highlights and urban attractions that gives the Mother City its unique flavour.

Foreshore and Heerengracht

The area known today as the **Foreshore** rests on what was once the beach and waters of Table Bay. In order to make way for the ever-expanding city, a considerable expanse of land was reclaimed from the sea in the late 1930s and early 1940s. Reclamation allowed the city to stretch from the City Bowl – the area encircled by Table Mountain, Lion's Head, Signal Hill, and Devil's Peak – to the new harbour, some two kilometres from its original shoreline. Down the centre of the Foreshore is the Heerengracht, the busy thoroughfare lined with towering office blocks, and dotted with fountains and statues of some of the city's founding fathers, including Portuguese explorer Bartolomeu Dias and Governor Jan van Riebeeck and his wife, Maria, as well as the War Memorial on Adderley Street.

Perhaps the most renowned of the structures on the Foreshore is the **Artscape Theatre Centre** on DF Malan Street. Erected in the late 1960s, the centre was opened in 1971 and remains one of the city's most important cultural centres, with an opera house and two theatres.

The **Cape Town International Convention Centre**, a stylish exhibition centre of mammoth proportions, which opened in 2003, includes within its ultramodern precincts the plush Westin Grand Hotel, galleries and exhibition halls, as well as two multi-seat auditoria that host a range of events and conferences on an international scale. From a bright and airy interior virtually glassed in by floor-to-ceiling windows is a spectacular view of the city and Table Mountain beyond.

PREVIOUS PAGES *Table Mountain, traditional landmark of Cape Town, watches over the twinkling lights of the city.*

INSET *Cape Town's venerable Lutheran Church seems like an island of the past amid the surrounding high-rise cityscape.*

ABOVE *The lively chatter of flower-sellers on Adderley Street is surpassed only by the vibrant colour of their bouquets.*

OPPOSITE *The handsome City Hall on Darling Street overlooks the Grand Parade.*

Hottentots-Holland Mountains

Cape Flats

Southern Suburbs

District Six

Civic Centre

Golden Acre

Railway Station

Castle of Good Hope

Greenmarket Square

Devil's Peak

City Bowl

Gardens

⬇ Houses of Parliament ⬇ Tuynhuys ⬇ Iziko South African National Gallery

⬆ National Library of South Africa Company's Garden Iziko South African Museum ⬆

Tourist Information

Cape Town Tourism is a consolidated tourism body that has successfully integrated a wide range of visitor facilities under a single umbrella. This valuable and exciting information service is proactive in developing the local infrastructure for the tourist market. The initiative represents a number of local publicity associations and specialised tour operators, and is devoted to marketing Cape Town to a worldwide audience. The website is updated regularly and packed with useful information, and the e-mail service is especially helpful in guiding prospective visitors as to choices in accommodation, tours, museums, tourist facilities and issues of safety.

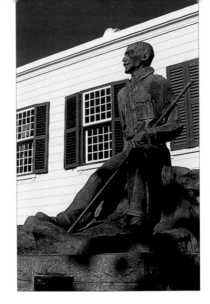

Adderley Street

Named in 1849 for Charles Adderley, the British politician who thwarted attempts by the Crown to turn the Cape into a convict station, **Adderley Street** – the upper half of the Heerengracht – is the city centre's main concourse – and forms the heart of Cape Town. Along its busy pavements are shops, businesses, hotels and apartment buildings, as well as the inimitable flower-sellers and street vendors who add both colour and life to the CBD. Here, too, is a statue of Vasco da Gama, the Portuguese sailor who first rounded the Cape of Good Hope in 1498 on his way to India. In December, the African-themed Christmas lights and a lively night market add a rainbow of colour and an air of festivity to the nightlife of Adderley Street.

One of the most imposing structures on Adderley Street is the gigantic **Golden Acre** shopping mall, which was erected in 1978 on the site of the old Customs buildings. As part of the Foreshore, black tiles laid into the floor indicate the original shoreline. Beneath the impressive domed skylight of the complex is a variety of stores, restaurants, banks and office suites, but visitors are warned that the crowds in and around the Golden Acre make it an ideal venue for pickpockets and petty thieves. Nevertheless, the parade of pedestrians can provide endless diversion. Within the walls of the complex is also a fascinating peek into the history of the Cape settlement. During construction of the Golden Acre, the site of the original stone dam erected by Governor Zacharias Wagenaer was uncovered, and is preserved behind glass on the lower level. A scale model indicates the location of the reservoir in relation to the plan of the early town.

Historical Cape Town

The **Groote Kerk**, overlooking both Church Square and upper Adderley Street, is the Mother Church of the Dutch Reformed Church and dates back to 1700, when Governor Willem Adriaan van der Stel laid the foundations for the new church. The Groote Kerk is noted for its fine architectural and sculptural features, particularly the extraordinary pulpit, which rests on a pedestal of lions, and was carved by sculptors Anton Anreith and Jan Graaff in 1789. The original building was replaced

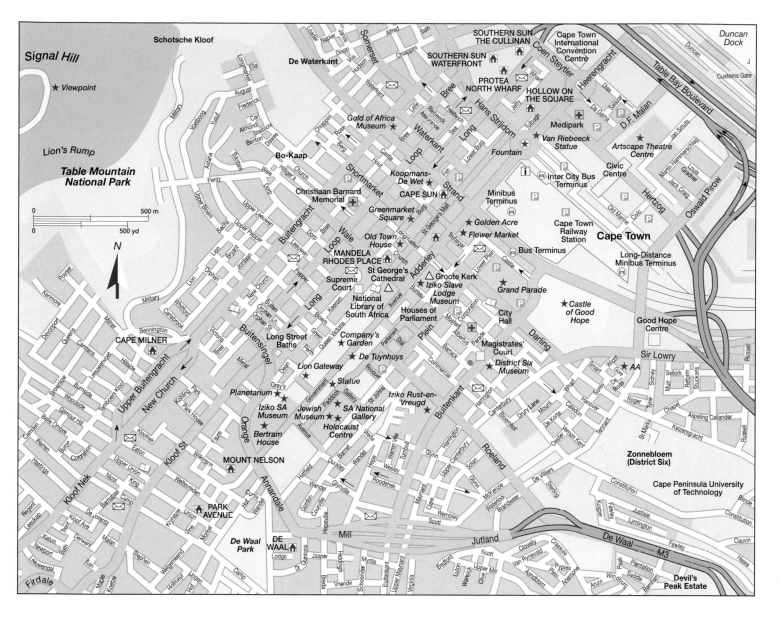

in 1841 by a Gothic-Egyptian structure. All that remains of the old church is the Baroque clock tower and steeple, and the tombstones that pave the floor. Modern facilities include a conference and visitors' centre.

PREVIOUS PAGES *Seen here from Signal Hill, the centre of Cape Town spreads across the City Bowl to the slopes of Devil's Peak.*

OPPOSITE TOP *The statue of General Jan Christiaan Smuts at the top of Adderley Street commemorates one of the country's most powerful historical figures.*

OPPOSITE BOTTOM *Shaded by grand old oaks, Government Avenue is a tranquil haven in the heart of the city.*

RIGHT *Grey squirrels indigenous to North America have scurried around the Company's Garden for more than a hundred years.*

Exciting innovations at the **Iziko Slave Lodge Museum** have elevated it from a series of conventional 'do not touch' exhibitions to a vibrant Memory Centre. The focus is on social history research into culture and identity, as well as contemporary socio-political developments. The museum aims to provide visitors with insight into the lives of those who were enslaved at the Cape during the period of the early settlement. Sections of the VOC slave lodge – which has served as a brothel and a Supreme Court at different times in its fascinating history – were designed by French architect Louis Thibault, and the pediment on the rear facade was sculpted by Anton Anreith.

Government Avenue and Beyond

A line of old oak trees separates tranquil **Government Avenue** from the stately Houses of Parliament,

Tuynhuys, the Iziko Slave Lodge Museum and the Iziko South African National Gallery, making the leafy pedestrian boulevard a favourite both for lunchtime strollers and the animated grey squirrels brought to the colony from North America by premier Cecil John Rhodes. Along the length of Government Avenue lie the six acres of the **Company's Garden**, originally laid out in 1652 by Jan van Riebeeck and his gardener, Hendrik Boom, as a vegetable garden to provide fresh supplies to the ships of the Dutch East India Company when they called at the Cape. Today, the garden is home to magnificent stands of both indigenous and exotic vegetation.

The imposing seat of South Africa's legislature, the **Houses of Parliament**, is situated on the east side of Government Avenue. The original design by Charles Freeman boasted porticos and pavilions and an impressive dome, which was modified by Henry Greaves to create the Victorian splendour we see today. Opened in 1884, the buildings include the Gallery Hall – containing portraits, sculptures, documents and other remnants of a bygone era. The galleries are open to the public while parliament is in session in the first six months of the year, and one-hour tours are conducted. Tours include a viewing of the public galleries and commentaries on parliamentary procedure.

Next to the Houses of Parliament is the President's city office, the Colonial Regency-style **Tuynhuys**, originally erected in the 17th-century to house visiting dignitaries. The building's eclectic appearance is the result of the many renovations carried out over the years. Although restored to its 1795 glory, Tuynhuys is closed to the public, but visitors can stroll along Government Avenue to admire its architectural splendour.

The **Iziko South African National Gallery**, in the Company's Garden on Government Avenue, is one of the highlights of a visit to Cape Town. The gallery exhibits South African and international paintings, sculptures, multimedia installations and crafts, as well as 17th-century Italian masters and contemporary photography. The gallery's permanent collection contains over 6 000 works of art, many of them bequeathed by Sir Abe Bailey, a local politician and businessman.

At the top end of Government Avenue, lies **Bertram House Museum**. The red-brick home of attorney-cum-builder John Barker is the city's only surviving brick Georgian house. The museum is a fine example of a British colonial home of the era, and exhibits include superb furniture and objets d'art from the Georgian, Queen Anne and Victorian periods. For admirers of more contemporary pursuits, Bertram House occasionally hosts music concerts, exhibitions, lectures and workshops – covering such diverse topics as painting, calligraphy and flower arranging. For information on facilities at the recently renovated precinct contact Iziko Museums.

Fronted on Queen Victoria Street by an equestrian statue commemorating the fallen heroes of both world wars, **Iziko South African Museum** is the country's oldest and most revered museum. Founded in 1825, the museum is today a constant reminder of the cultural and natural heritage of South Africa and, indeed, the world. Favourite drawcards include the dinosaurs and other fossil displays. Cultural development is traced through artefacts as diverse as rock paintings and stone implements to items brought back from the Pacific Islands by explorer Captain James Cook.

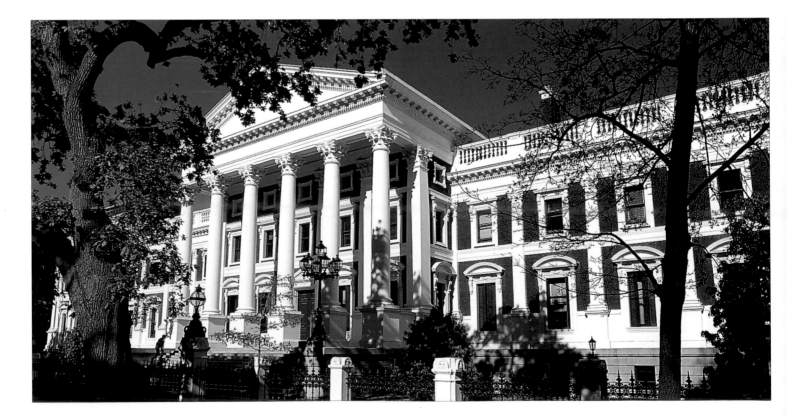

Apart from the presentations on archaeology and geology, the exhibitions on Africa's natural history include reproductions of birds, fish and other wildlife. The most impressive is the **Whale Well**. The four-level whale exhibit includes the massive skeleton and jaw bones of a blue whale. You can also listen to the whale song of the humpback in the yellow submersible.

No visit to the Iziko South African Museum is complete without a stop at the **Planetarium,** housed under the same roof as the museum complex. This fascinating look into the night skies of the southern hemisphere is so popular that visitors are advised to make reservations for one of the many shows offered daily. Features include a look at the changing constellations of the past, present and future, covering more than 25 000 years. Public lectures explore issues such as new frontiers in space exploration and, for the younger set, there is a talking robotic astronaut and fantastic laser shows.

The neighbouring **Great Synagogue** and **South African Jewish Museum** were designed by Scotsmen Parker and Forsythe. The Baroque opulence of the Synagogue, consecrated in 1905, is most notable for its impressive dome and twin towers, and remains a marvel of architecture. Alongside the Great Synagogue is the Old Synagogue. Of Egyptian-Revival design, it was the first to be built in the colony, and was opened in 1863. Today, the Old Synagogue houses the historical and ceremonial treasures of the Jewish Museum. The **Cape Town Holocaust Centre** is the only such complex in Africa. This is not only a memorial to Jews persecuted in Nazi Germany, but also a haunting reminder of the effects of racial prejudice and discrimination.

At the top of Government Avenue is Orange Street, which becomes Mill Street to the east and Annandale Street to the west, and then leads into Buitensingel and Long Street. It is along Orange Street that visitors will encounter the elegant old **Mount Nelson Hotel**, one of the finest hotels the city has to offer. The colonial grace of what is affectionately known as 'The Nellie', has played host to royalty, movie stars, statesmen

OPPOSITE *The grand exterior of the Houses of Parliament has remained relatively unchanged since the early 1900s.*

TOP RIGHT *The equestrian memorial outside the Iziko South African Museum is one of many dotted throughout the city centre.*

UPPER MIDDLE RIGHT *The leafy Company's Garden is the perfect place to take a break from a hectic day of sightseeing.*

LOWER MIDDLE RIGHT *The skeleton of a blue whale dominates the cavernous Whale Well at the Iziko South African Museum.*

BOTTOM RIGHT *Affectionately known as 'The Nellie', the gracious old Mount Nelson Hotel at the top of the Gardens has for decades been a favoured stayover for affluent travellers.*

William Fehr Collection – the remainder may be viewed at the Castle of Good Hope. Beyond the filigreed iron gates, pillared porch and the Baroque doorway carved by Anton Anreith is one of the finest collections of period objets d'art in the country, varying from furniture to Old Masters, and including a number of works by the noted landscape artist, Thomas Baines. There is also an art gallery with paintings for sale to the public, and a formal herb and rose garden that recreates a typical Dutch garden of the early Cape.

At the lower end of Buitenkant Street stands the imposing **Castle of Good Hope**, the oldest surviving – and occupied – building in South Africa. Built between 1666 and 1679, this pentagonal fortification, with its stately gateway, was constructed out of timber brought from Hout Bay, stone quarried on Robben Island and lime burnt from seashells. Overlooking the city's **Grand Parade** – the site of Van Riebeeck's original fort – the Castle serves primarily as a museum and the headquarters of the South African National Defence Force's Western Province Command. Within its fortified walls are both the **Good Hope Gallery** and the **Military Museum** – housing an array of military artefacts and uniforms covering both the Dutch and British periods of occupation.

The five bastions of the star-shaped Castle were named after the main titles of Wilhelm, Prince of Orange: Leerdam, Buuren, Catzenellenbogen, Nassau and Oranje. The thick stone walls encompass the original armoury, dungeon, kitchen, barracks, prison, church, cellars and servants' quarters. The entrance fee allows visitors to join hourly guided tours, which take in the lovely **Dolphin Pool**, and to see either the opening Ceremony of the Keys or the Changing of the Guard at noon.

In 1695, a wall boasting an impressive balcony – known as 'De Kat' – was built across the Castle courtyard for extra defence. This projecting verandah facing the main courtyard gives access to the large audience chamber, and is one of the Castle's architectural gems. Inside are fine examples of paintings, decorative arts and period furniture of the **William Fehr Collection**. The displays are of special relevance to the Cape and its history, and are housed in what was once the Governor's Quarters and the council chambers of the Dutch East India Company (VOC).

Darling Street

The **Grand Parade** was once a military parade ground, but is now the site of the country's oldest market. The market area has for years been a trading emporium for informal vendors and casual shoppers. In 2009, the square underwent a dramatic facelift initiated by a local business initiative intent on revitalising the heart of the city, most especially in preparation for the 2010 Soccer World Cup™. It was on the Grand Parade

and politicians, and remains the epitome of charm and sophistication. Visitors cannot find a better venue for afternoon tea or a light lunch. Although it is rather expensive, the luxury and service remain unsurpassed. For fine dining, visit the exceptional Cape Colony restaurant, or stop off for cocktails in the swish Planet Champagne Bar.

The area around Government Avenue, stretching from the **Gardens** area all the way down to **Cape Heritage Square** in the CBD proper, has become a mecca for connoisseurs of fun, fine food and good wines, and a number of acclaimed restaurants and bars have sprung up in many of the old residential homes. On Heritage Square, mingle with the young and trendy at Savoy Cabbage or Caveau, or feast on a selection of African cuisine from around the continent at the Africa Café. Alternatively, make your way up **Kloof Street**, where you can sample Mediterranean dishes at Café Paradiso, exquisite Vietnamese fare at Saigon, the delights of the swanky new Opal Lounge, and fine fusion food with a twist at the funky new Bombay Bicycle Club.

Buitenkant Street
At 78 Buitenkant Street stands the 18th-century **Iziko Rust-en-Vreugd** manor house, which houses part of the historical

in 1990 that 250 000 supporters gathered to welcome Nelson Mandela after his release from 27 years in prison. Mandela addressed the throng from the balcony of the **City Hall**, the Italian Renaissance building of granite and marble on the opposite side of Darling Street. Designed by Harry Austin Reid and Frederick George Green, City Hall was officially opened to the people of Cape Town in 1905; the tower was added in 1923. The hall's main chamber boasts an organ with more than 3 000 pipes, and occasionally hosts concerts by the Cape Philharmonic Orchestra. Bookings for these recitals may be made through Computicket.

Beyond the Castle, on Oswald Pirow Street, is the distinctive grey dome of the **Good Hope Centre**, designed by the Italian architect Pier Luigi Nervi. The Good Hope Centre is a popular venue for concerts, sports tournaments and trade fairs, as well as

a meeting place for sociopolitical organisations. Parking here is at a premium and visitors are warned that car theft is a serious problem and valuables should never be left unattended.

District Six

Visitors to the city will notice that nestling in the embrace of the mountain is a vacant stretch of land punctuated only by a few buildings. The **Moravian Chapel** – once a mission station and now a sports centre for the nearby Cape Peninsula University of Technology – and a mosque are practically all that remains of the once thriving community of **District Six**. Under the apartheid laws, the 'coloured' families who lived and worked in the area were relocated to outlying townships, and the entire neighbourhood was bulldozed to the ground. With the co-operation of its original inhabitants and their families, the area has recently been earmarked for community development. Today, a number of brand-new homes – many in the simple architectural styles of the original houses that dotted the mountainside – are already springing up on the mostly open, weed-covered veld. Plans are afoot to add to the existing housing scheme and to redevelop the infrastructure. **The District Six Museum**, housed in the former Methodist Mission in Buitenkant Street, has been called in to help oversee the authenticity of the redevelopment.

Strand Street

One of the most significant buildings on historic Strand Street – so named because it ran along the 'strand', or beach

---

Opposite Top *The pentagonal Castle of Good Hope, originally on the shoreline, was erected to defend the early Dutch colony.*

Opposite Bottom *The cool galleries of the Castle preserve stately reminders of the British and Dutch occupations of the Cape.*

Above *The District Six Museum offers a glimpse into the lives of those who inhabited this once vibrant neighbourhood before being forcibly removed under apartheid laws.*

Heart of the Mother City

– is **Koopmans-De Wet House**, a splendid period home. This 18th-century townhouse, with its cobbled courtyard and flagstone floors, was the home of human rights campaigner and Cape socialite Maria de Wet (1838–1906), widow of Johan Koopmans, who bequeathed it to the state on her death. The house was built in 1701 by VOC official Reynier Smedinga and later renovated by the famed masters, Louis Thibault and Anton Anreith. The museum houses a fine collection of furniture and household items collected by Maria de Wet and her sister.

Strand Street's other stately old building is the **Lutheran Church**. Because religious toleration was limited in the Cape during the 1700s, Martin Melck opened his barn to parishioners. This humble structure was then converted into a church, featuring a façade by Anton Anreith, who also executed the work on both the organ loft and the exquisite pulpit depicting the Lutheran symbol of the swan.

De Waterkant

Just below Strand Street, stretching across the lower slopes of Signal Hill, is an area that once housed a close-knit, largely coloured community – tailors and seamstresses, craftsmen and artisans, shopkeepers and drivers – banished from the more affluent suburbs and central business district. Somewhat rundown and neglected over the years, the modest homes squeezed tightly along narrow streets nevertheless retained a certain charm. The result was that the zone, more or less demarcated by Buitengracht and Boundary, Somerset and Strand streets, is now prime real estate much sought after by property investors. Like so many of the office blocks in the city centre that have seen redevelopment as 'inner-city living', the area now known as De Waterkant has emerged as one of the most prestigious in the city and among the most charming. The simple, single-storey homes have evolved into sophisticated

multi-storey complexes, painstakingly – and at great expense – upgraded for a modern urban lifestyle. Scattered among these up-market residences are bistros and boutiques, clubs and restaurants – all known for their celebration of 'the good life'.

Greenmarket Square

One of Cape Town's top tourist attractions, **Greenmarket Square** lies at the intersection of Longmarket and Burg streets. The square at the heart of the city's business district started out as a market in 1710, a place where fruit and vegetable growers marketed their wares, and farmers brought wagons laden with

OPPOSITE TOP *Greenmarket Square is Cape Town's most popular outdoor market and never fails to delight both visitors and locals.*

OPPOSITE BOTTOM LEFT *Renovation at De Waterkant has seen careful integration of the old facades into the contemporary architecture.*

OPPOSITE BOTTOM RIGHT *Today, De Waterkant is an exciting blend of commercial activity and residential charm.*

ABOVE LEFT *Church Street is the informal home of the city's antique trade and a genuine find may occasionally be discovered among the bric-a-brac.*

ABOVE RIGHT *Charming pavement bistros punctuate the quaint Church Street Mall.*

produce to sell to the town folk. Today, the quaint square has returned to its original use, and is filled every day – except Sunday – with funky market stalls carrying virtually anything from clothing, curios, collectibles and crafts to artwork, jewellery, books, leatherware and other fine treasures amid the obligatory curios and tourist souvenirs. Saturday mornings see the recently renovated cobbled square packed with shoppers feverishly picking through the numerous bargains on offer. The patchwork of bright, umbrella-shaded trading stalls heavy with bric-a-brac, junk and, occasionally, genuine antiques, adds colour and life to the central business district. Naturally, prices are subject to discussion, and haggling is part of the passing parade of entertainment. Girding the small square are several very attractive buildings. Home to the city's first police force, the **Old Town House** – erected in the late 1750s – houses under its star-spangled dome the famed Michaelis Art Collection of outstanding Dutch and Flemish masters of the 17th century. The Gothic Revival style of the **Metropolitan Methodist Church**, with its ornate entrance on Burg Street, is a Victorian masterpiece designed by Charles Freeman.

Church Street

For the bargain hunter or antique enthusiast, the quaint pedestrian mall in Church Street may offer a rare find. The genuine items are more often than not to be found within some of the street's shops, while the pavements of Church, Burg and Long streets are packed with the stuff grandmother just forgot to throw out. Nevertheless, there may be one or two choice pieces and the stallholders are always willing to help with

Heart of the Mother City

your purchase of a porcelain plate, Victorian jewel or brass and pewter knick-knacks. The setting of delightfully old buildings and ornamental balconies is particularly appropriate to the bargaining taking place in the streets below.

Long Street

The famed **Long Street** – known throughout the city for its magnificent old edifices and charming bookshops – is more than 300 years old, and reflects all the allure of a bygone era. Today, Capetonians motor past old Orphan House, where the University of Cape Town held its first lectures, and up the – quite literally – long street, which once saw minstrels entertaining passers-by, and where produce vendors sold their wares from barrows. Nowadays Long Street is lined with bars, backpacker establishments and chic eateries popular with the fashionable crowd. It is also home to the **Pan African Market**, which boasts a vast collection of authentic African arts and crafts, and with over 30 stalls competing for your custom you are guaranteed to find a bargain. Long Street's architectural features include Georgian, Victorian, Cape Malay and 20th-century styles.

The Palm Tree Mosque, which is the second oldest mosque in Cape Town, was converted into a mosque in 1807 by Jan van Boughies, himself a slave who had been granted his freedom.

Further up are the **Long Street Baths** – comprising a swimming pool, Turkish baths, steam rooms for either men or women (depending on the day) – and a number of unique shops and bookstores, such as **Clarke's Bookshop**, which sell antiquarian books and Africana.

Behind the doors of the 1804 church near the corner of Hout and Long streets is the **Slave Church Museum**, which

chronicles the Sendinggestig – Dutch for 'Mission Foundation' – established in the early 19th century by evangelists from the London and Netherlands missionary societies to bring Christianity to the slaves. The building contains a fine pulpit, pipe organ and displays on the history of missionary work at the Cape. The floors are of Robben Island slate, while the galleries are carved from indigenous yellowwood and stinkwood and the pews from imported American oak.

TOP LEFT *As darkness settles, Long Street – heart of the city's nightlife – comes alive, filling up with partygoers on the prowl.*

ABOVE *Acclaimed for its architectural splendour, Long Street is lined with beautifully ornate Victorian structures.*

LEFT *The rhythmic movements of a traditional Zulu dancer in St George's Mall attracts delighted onlookers.*

OPPOSITE TOP *Neat rows of old Cape cottages line the steeply sloping streets of the Bo-Kaap, the traditional home of the Muslim community.*

OPPOSITE INSET *From an unusual vantage point, a young resident provides his own directions to the Bo-Kaap.*

St George's Mall and Wale Street

The pedestrian concourse of **St George's Mall**, fringed with shops, arcades, kiosks and eateries, is a hive of activity, with street musicians providing informal entertainment and vendors plying their trade. Overlooking the mall, the signature hotel **Mandela Rhodes Place** is the place to be. It's a vibrant inner-city social hub, with a fine restaurant. In the same complex– just around the corner in Church Street – is the **Rainbow Room**, one of the city's most exciting and vibrant jazz venues. At the top of the mall, on the other side of Wale Street, is the Gothic **St George's Cathedral**, built on the site of the original cathedral consecrated in 1848, and replaced in 1897 by the new design of

Sir Herbert Baker and Francis Massey. This was the home parish of Nobel laureate Desmond Tutu, the former Anglican Archbishop of Cape Town. The awe-inspiring cathedral boasts the lovely stained-glass Rose Window by Francis Spear, and the 8-metre (24 feet) window depicting early Anglican saints and pioneers. The Treasury houses a list of over 27 000 British soldiers who died in the South African War. Services are held at St George's at 11am on the last Sunday of the month, and choral music is regularly performed.

Behind the cathedral is the **National Library of South Africa**. Modelled on the Fitzwilliam Museum at Cambridge University, the dazzling white building houses important reference works. Nearby is the affiliated – and impressive – **Centre for the Book**.

Back on Wale Street, at number 71, is the **Iziko Bo-Kaap Museum**. The building dates back to 1760 and was once owned by Abu Bakr Effendi, a scholar who published one of the first books in Afrikaans. The house is furnished in the style of a 19th-century Muslim home, with a collection of photographs and personal effects. The museum is also the starting point for walking tours of the **Bo-Kaap**, which give a unique insight into the fascinating and historically rich district.

USEFUL INFORMATION

CAPE TOWN TOURISM

Cape Town Tourism manages tourism across the greater city area, its network of well-positioned Visitor Information Centres specialising in offering sound advice on accommodation, tours, vehicle hire, transport facilities, dining out, sport and adventure, and other reliable travel tips. It also facilitates communication between member organisations aimed at improving service levels and helps establish standards and norms for the local hospitality industry. Contact **Cape Town Tourism** at the V&A Waterfront Gateway Information Office, info@tourismcapetown.co.za; tel: 021 405-4500; www.tourismcapetown.co.za, and **Cape Town Routes Unlimited**, tel: 021 487-4800. Search for a museum online at **www.museums.org.za**

Artscape Theatre Centre: DF Malan St, Foreshore; tel: 021 410-9800; www.artscape.co.za
Bertram House: Hiddingh Campus, cnr Orange St/Government Ave; open 10am–5pm, Mon and Fri only; tel: 021 481-3940, 021 424-9381
Cape Town International Convention Centre: Convention Sq, Lower Long St; tel: 021 410-5000; www.capetownconvention.com
Castle of Good Hope: Castle St; open 9am–4pm daily; tel: 021 787-1260; www.castleofgoodhope.co.za
City Hall: Darling St; open 7am–4pm daily; tel: 021 465-2029
Clarke's Bookshop: 211 Long St; tel: 021 423-5739
Company's Garden: Botanical gardens; open daily 9.30am–4pm
District Six Museum: 25a Buitenkant St; open 9am–4pm Mon–Sat; tel: 021 461-8745; www.districtsix.co.za
Gold of Africa Museum: Martin Melck House, 96 Strand St; open 9.30am–5pm Mon–Sat; tel: 021 405-1540; www.goldofafrica.com
Good Hope Centre: Sir Lowry Rd; tel: 021 465-4688
Great Synagogue, Jewish Museum and **Holocaust Centre:** 88 Hatfield St, Gardens; 10am–5pm Sun–Thurs, 10am–2pm Fri; tel: 021 465-1546
Groote Kerk: Adderley St; open daily 10.30am–12pm, 2pm–3pm
Houses of Parliament: Parliament St; open for tours 9am–12pm, Mon–Fri; tel: 021 403-2911, 021 403-2266
Iziko Bo-Kaap Museum: 71 Wale St; open 10am–5pm
Iziko Rust-en-Vreugd: 78 Buitenkant St; open 8.30am–4.30pm Tues–Thurs; tel: 021 464-3280
Iziko Slave Lodge Museum: 49 Adderley St; open 10am–4.30pm Mon–Sat; tel: 021 460-8200
Iziko South African Museum: Queen Victoria St; open daily 10am–5pm; tel: 021 481-3800
Iziko South African National Gallery: Company's Garden; open 10am–5pm Tues–Sun; tel: 021 467-4660
Koopmans-De Wet House: 35 Strand St; open 9am–4pm Tues–Thurs; tel: 021 481-3935
Old Town House (Michaelis Art Collection): Greenmarket Sq; 10am–5pm Mon–Fri, 10am–4pm Sat; tel: 021 481-3933
Pan African Market: 76 Long St; open 9am–5pm Mon–Fri, 9am–3pm Sat; tel: 021 426-4478
Planetarium: Queen Victoria St; screenings 2pm Mon–Fri, 8pm Tues, 12pm, 1pm and 2.30pm Sat–Sun; tel: 021 481-3900
Sendinggestig Museum: 40 Long St; open 9am–4pm Mon–Fri; tel: 021 423-6755
St George's Cathedral: Wale St; open daily 8am–6pm; tel: 021 424-7360; www.stgeorgescathedral.com
Westin Grand Hotel, Cape Town: Convention Sq, Lower Long St; tel: 021 412-9999, 0800 994 276; www.westin.com/capetown

DAY 2

THE V&A WATERFRONT
& ROBBEN ISLAND

THE V&A WATERFRONT & ROBBEN ISLAND

Victoria Wharf • Victoria Basin • Alfred Basin • The Pierhead • The Clock Tower Precinct
Table Bay • Two Oceans Aquarium • Robben Island

In recent years, beginning in the early 1990s, Cape Town has been at the centre of an unprecedented development boom, and nowhere has this been more evident than in the vicinity of Table Bay. When Prince Alfred, eldest son of Queen Victoria, inaugurated the Alfred Basin in 1860, few could imagine that the simple jetty would evolve into today's V&A Waterfront complex – a working harbour and shopping and entertainment mecca. The revitalised dockland, set against the backdrop of Table Mountain, is now a leisure wonderland, and has become the country's premier tourist attraction.

Victoria Wharf

Although the **V&A Waterfront** is relatively close to the central business district of Cape Town, it is not easily accessible on foot – walking from the CBD to the harbour means crossing busy main streets. Buses – both municipal and dedicated Waterfront shuttles – leave fairly regularly from the Adderley Street exit of the city railway station, and ferry visitors to the Waterfront. Whether arriving via the Waterfront Shuttle service or municipal

bus, commuters alight at the entrance to the chic **Victoria Wharf** on Breakwater Boulevard leading to the East Pier. The bright and airy glass-topped mall is a stylish combination of up-market shopping experiences, fashionable eateries and an absorbing parade of both locals and visitors. The complex of converted warehouses houses a cornucopia of fine food, exquisite (and rather pricey) artefacts, and elegant designerwear. Also included within its galleries are cinemas, office suites, an automated banking hall and a post office. Be sure to stop for breakfast or a light lunch at one of the mall's many restaurants, such as Balducci's or Mugg & Bean, or dine at the house restaurants of the swish hotels such as Cape Grace, The Table Bay and The Commodore. Within the mall itself, you will find even more coffee shops and fast-food outlets, serving everything from pizza slices to sushi and shwarmas. Nearby is the **V&A Waterfront Amphitheatre**, an intimate open-air venue in the heart of the complex that hosts a wide variety of entertainers, and is especially popular on sultry summer evenings when the music wafts on the gentle sea breeze.

PREVIOUS PAGES *Quay Four and Quay Five in the Victoria Basin form a hub of entertainment at the V&A Waterfront.*

INSET *Age-old inhabitants of the old harbour continue to make their home on the revitalised docks.*

ABOVE *A nighttime panorama of the Waterfront complex shows the new basin in the foreground.*

OPPOSITE *The steel and glass facade of the Victoria Wharf shopping mall echoes the shapes of the warehouses of the old docks.*

Table Mountain

The Twelve Apostles

Lion's Head

Cape Town CBD

De Waterkant

Waterfront Residential Marina

New Basin

Cape Grace Hotel

Iziko Maritime Centre

Alfred Basin

Nelson Mandela Gateway ⬇

The Pierhead ⬆

The Clock Tower ⬆

Victoria Basin

Signal Hill

Sea Point

Green Point

One&Only

← Graduate School of Business

← Breakwater Lodge

← Two Oceans Aquarium

← Portswood Complex

Cape Town Stadium

■ Waterfront Craft Market

← Somerset Hospital

Victoria & Alfred Hotel

← The Pavilion Conference Centre

↓ King's Warehouse

ay Five

Granger Bay ➡

Victoria Wharf

Table Bay Hotel

Below Victoria Wharf, on Quay Five, are a few popular late-night party and dinner venues, as well as the landing dock for the pleasure boats offering charters and trips into Table Bay harbour and beyond to the leisure strip of the Atlantic seaboard.

Markets for Africa

If shopping is high on your list of priorities, however, leave Victoria Wharf via the adjoining **King's Warehouse** on the southwest end of the complex. Food fundis will find stalls purveying fresh fish, ethnic specialities and fast foods. Beyond this lively emporium, visitors will find the **Red Shed**, an eclectic mix of art, craft, textiles and jewellery, as well as an array of traditional African basketware, beadwork and township art. Of particular note among the offerings of more than 20 speciality craft stalls is the glass-blowing demonstration. The rear exit from the Red Shed leads to the popular **Ferryman's Tavern**, part of the converted warehouses housing Mitchell's Brewery, which offers a range of beers brewed on the premises.

Market Square and Surrounds

Opposite the Ferryman's Tavern is gravelled **Market Square** – a venue for outdoor exhibitions and performances throughout the year – bordered by the impressive collection of wines at **Vaughan Johnson's Wine Shop**. The selection here is among the best in the city, and staff can arrange for cases of the Cape's finest wines to be shipped home. Across the square is **Quay Four**, a pub-cum-restaurant nestled right on Victoria Basin. This is a lively spot and the action continues well into the night.

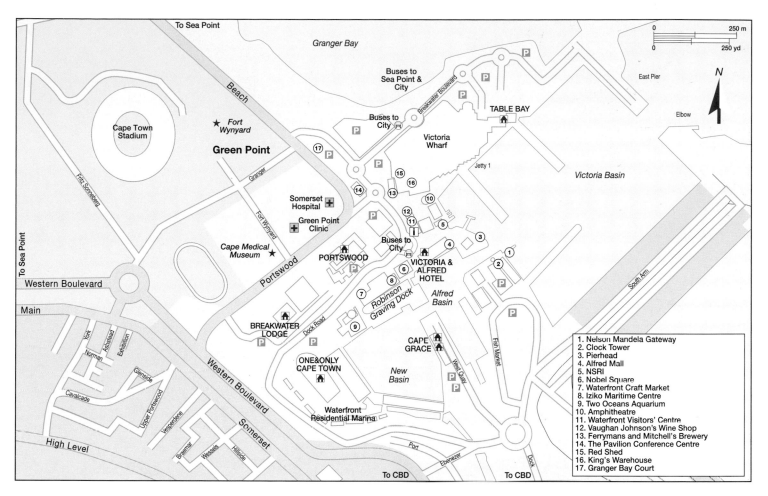

The Pierhead & Surrounds

In your excitement to take in everything the Waterfront has to offer, be sure to take some time to browse around the **Pierhead**, a small extension of the harbour overlooking both Victoria Basin and the entrance to Alfred Basin. This shopping and entertainment enclave offers superb views across Victoria Basin. In and around the Pierhead there is a variety of top-of-the-range shopping venues, including international brand names such as Dunhill, Paul Smith, Jimmy Choo, Hugo Boss, Gucci and Guess Kids. There are also plenty of bistros, coffee shops and restaurants, including the Hildebrand and the swanky Alba Lounge. One or two of the curio shops are also worth a browse. Street entertainers and buskers on the Pierhead provide a pleasant diversion from shopping, eating and walking. These musicians and mime artists – some of them exceptionally talented – add a unique local flavour to the Waterfront complex.

PREVIOUS PAGES *A gull's-eye view shows the expansive V&A Waterfront and adjoining docklands.*

OPPOSITE TOP *Costumed minstrels with painted faces entertain the crowds as part of the annual New Year festivities.*

OPPOSITE MIDDLE *The V&A Waterfront Amphitheatre off Market Square hosts lively open-air musical performances.*

OPPOSITE BOTTOM *Buskers are a welcome addition to the charm of the Pierhead.*

RIGHT *Amid the profusion of shops and eateries, children delight in the traditional carousel off Market Square.*

The Clock Tower Precinct

The redevelopment of the area surrounding the old Clock Tower was finalised in 2001. This once rather dilapidated area of the docks is now one of its most innovative, boasting a host of new attractions and facilities. The rejuvenation project is centred around the office space for high-flying corporates, the historic **Clock Tower** itself and the **Nelson Mandela Gateway**, quite literally the 'gateway' to the famed island prison in Table Bay. The upgraded facilities, which have helped facilitate the ever-increasing number of visitors to Robben Island, include the **Robben Island Museum**, as well as the passenger ferry terminal to the island itself. As the headquarters of the Robben Island Museum, the Gateway complex houses both the offices and exhibition halls, as well as a shop and restaurant. The most significant drawcard of the three-storeyed glass building is, however, the 150-seat auditorium that forms its focus.

Maritime History – the Floating Exhibits

As you walk towards the mountain, straight ahead lies the **Alfred Basin**, in which two floating exhibits are permanently moored. The SAS *Somerset* is the only remaining boom defence ship in the world – although no longer open to public viewing

– while the *Alwyn Vincent* is a steam tug. Both exhibits are satellites of the **Iziko Maritime Centre** just a few metres away, next to the cavernous Blue Shed that houses the Waterfront Craft Market. Museum exhibits include the largest collection of model ships in the country, a view of a shipwright's workshop, a children's discovery cove and a shipwreck display.

Hospitality on the Water

Before you reach the crafts centre, however, you will almost certainly be struck by the much-photographed blue-and-white **Victoria & Alfred Hotel**, which has become a landmark in the Waterfront. On the lower level, the acclaimed hotel boasts the **Alfred Mall**, which concentrates largely on exclusive jewellery and curios, one or two coffee shops offering light snacks and refreshments, and the popular **Green Dolphin Restaurant**, which is renowned for both its fine food and live jazz.

Top among the Waterfront's complement of five-star hotels along the water's edge are the elegant **Cape Grace** (often the Cape Town base of international luminaries, including state leaders, politicians and a host of movie stars and musicians), **The Table Bay** and the magnificent new **One&Only**, Cape Town's top resort complex. All are architectural landmarks, and their cuisine, vintage wines and dramatic vistas of both the Atlantic and the brooding mountain represent the ultimate in luxury. Little wonder that they are the chosen stopovers of celebrities.

A variation to the many eateries on the Waterfront is the floating restaurant, *The Sea Horse*, a pleasure boat that offers an exciting alternative to an evening's entertainment on the waters of Table Bay and surrounds. This is the most famous of what are, not entirely accurately, called 'booze cruises', although a number of other similar-style but smaller vessels offer excursions out into the bay and beyond. These generally depart from Quay Five and, during the peak holiday season, they can be rather pricey.

The New Basin

Attractions on the water's edge of the new basin between Dock Road and Alfred Basin include an engaging mix of new and old. The **Robinson Graving Dock**, one of four working dry docks built on reclaimed land, is used to carry out vital repairs to vessels large and small. One of the harbour's most thrilling

sights is when sea water is pumped into the dock so that a rejuvenated vessel can float back out to sea. These occasions, however, are infrequent, as ships may stay in dry dock for months on end. It may be far more worthwhile to cross the **Bascule Bridge** to see the majestic Cape Grace Hotel on the West Quay. Beyond this gracious structure there is little of interest for the visitor as the quay leads into the working harbour, much of which is closed to the public.

Back on the west rim of the basin, however, is one of the Waterfront's most visited attractions. The Blue Shed houses the **Waterfront Craft Market**, with stall after stall of arts and crafts, and a boundless array of handwork, curios and memorabilia for the enthusiastic shopper. Although some of the local wares may be quite costly – stallholders inevitably cater for the well-heeled tourist market – they tend to be wonderfully creative and colourful, and offer a little of Africa to take home.

The Two Oceans Aquarium

One of the most popular additions to the V&A Waterfront is the world-class **Two Oceans Aquarium**, a marine wonderland with transparent underwater tunnels, a touch pool and tanks that hold a fascinating array of marine life found along the Atlantic and Indian Ocean coasts of southern Africa. Displays include prismatic tropical fish, a look at the ancient coelacanth, a shark tank, a seal tank opening onto the adjacent basin and the Open Ocean exhibit – two million litres of sea water that is home to creatures both great and small. The aquarium complex also houses a classroom and gift shop, and the aquarium's own Shoreline Café, a serene and laid-back pit stop that boasts an extensive children's menu as well as a play area for the kids.

Dock Road

From the aquarium, cross Dock Road – the heart of the old harbour and once notorious as the favourite haunt of 'ladies of the night' – to reach the **Portswood complex**, on the southern boundary of which is the **Breakwater Lodge**. Originally a prison, built in the mid-1800s to hold the convicts engaged in building the original docks, the reasonably priced hotel boasts 300 rooms for guests looking for interesting accommodation. The premises are also home to the Graduate School of Business, a satellite campus of the University of Cape Town. Next door, looking towards the ocean, is **Portswood Ridge**, a plush modern development of office suites and a parking arcade. Behind it is **The Portswood Hotel**, overlooking Portswood Road, which leads back into the city.

Directly below The Portswood on Dock Road may be found the treasures of the **Scratch Patch**. Young children – and even

some adults – will delight in uncovering the semi-precious stones hidden among the rocks and pebbles. Parents pay by weight for those stones that their children may want to take home. A few steps further on are **Dock House** and the **Time Ball Tower**, once used by passing ships to set their clocks. Buses to and from the city stop on this block, and on Alfred Square directly opposite, outside the Victoria & Alfred Hotel. Across Dock Road is **The Forum** conference venue and the **Visitors' Centre**, which handles all inquiries and reservations for some of the facilities available at the Waterfront.

The Residential Marina

When the V&A Waterfront was initially conceptualised in the late 1980s, the intention was to develop the dockland into not only a leisure and shopping destination for tourists and locals, but – in the tradition of similar ventures in Europe and the USA – also a prime residential zone boasting designer finishes, top-of-the-range facilities and, of course, some of the most

---

ABOVE *Huge windows and hands-on displays at the Two Oceans Aquarium make it a popular attraction for young and old.*

LEFT *Always on the lookout for a free meal, Cape fur seals are often seen basking on Seals' Landing adjacent to Bertie's Landing.*

OPPOSITE *Since Robben Island was opened to the public, ferries carry hundreds of visitors daily to the island reserve.*

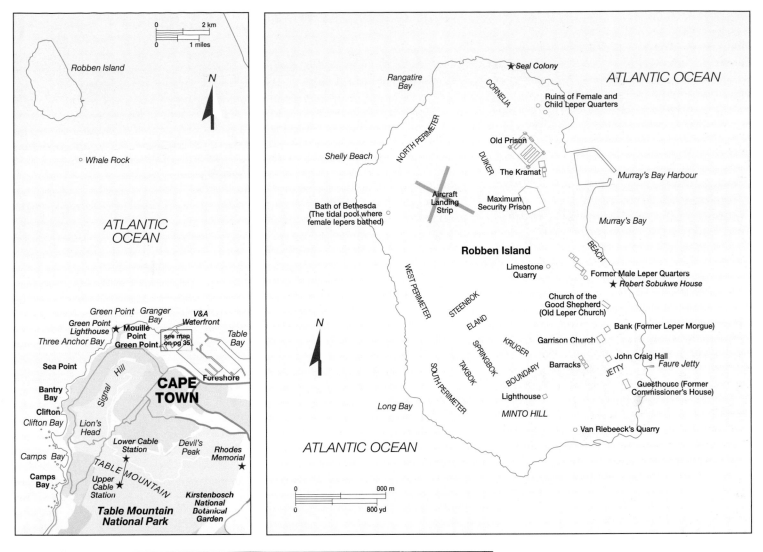

Map of Cape Town area

- Robben Island
- Whale Rock
- ATLANTIC OCEAN
- Green Point
- Granger Bay
- Green Point Lighthouse
- Mouille Point
- Three Anchor Bay
- Green Point
- V&A Waterfront
- see map on pg 35
- Table Bay
- Sea Point
- Signal Hill
- CAPE TOWN
- Foreshore
- Bantry Bay
- Clifton
- Lion's Head
- Clifton Bay
- Lower Cable Station
- Devil's Peak
- Rhodes Memorial
- Camps Bay
- TABLE MOUNTAIN
- Camps Bay
- Upper Cable Station
- Kirstenbosch National Botanical Garden
- Table Mountain National Park

Map of Robben Island

- Seal Colony
- Rangatire Bay
- CORNELIA
- ATLANTIC OCEAN
- Ruins of Female and Child Leper Quarters
- NORTH PERIMETER
- Shelly Beach
- DUIKER
- Old Prison
- The Kramat
- Murray's Bay Harbour
- Aircraft Landing Strip
- Maximum Security Prison
- Bath of Bethesda (The tidal pool where female lepers bathed)
- Murray's Bay
- BEACH
- Robben Island
- WEST PERIMETER
- Limestone Quarry
- Former Male Leper Quarters
- Robert Sobukwe House
- STEENBOK
- ELAND
- Church of the Good Shepherd (Old Leper Church)
- Bank (Former Leper Morgue)
- SPRINGBOK
- KRUGER
- Garrison Church
- TAKBOK
- BOUNDARY
- Barracks
- John Craig Hall
- JETTY
- Faure Jetty
- Long Bay
- SOUTH PERIMETER
- Lighthouse
- MINTO HILL
- Guesthouse (Former Commissioner's House)
- ATLANTIC OCEAN
- Van Riebeeck's Quarry

remarkable views from anywhere in the city. While this plan took more than a decade to implement, it rapidly began to take shape from about 2000 and the magnificent structures that have since sprung up around the semicircular basin make it one of the most sought-after addresses in the city. Naturally, the luxurious and decadent comforts, breathtaking interiors, magnificent sea vistas and unsurpassed view of majestic Table Mountain come at a cost, and the pricing of many of these up-market units, most used almost exclusively as holiday pads by foreign visitors, puts them beyond the reach of many locals.

Table Bay

With all these enticements on offer, one would think that there is little more to do at the Waterfront than to eat, shop or put your feet up and relax with a

the epic Volvo Ocean Race, which usually reaches the Cape Town leg in about early November. The arrival of the vessels launches an entire programme of waterfront entertainment that centres around the sailing extravaganza.

On the Waters

Apart from the Waterfront historical walk, details of which are available from the Visitors' Centre, the complex offers an assortment of mini-tours and excursions. Among the most popular offerings from the charter companies operating from the harbour are round-the-harbour boat trips, twilight cruises, and even game-fishing expeditions. Quay Four and Quay Five in the Victoria Basin offer boat charters and cruise trips into Table Bay – and even around to Clifton and other spots along the Atlantic seaboard. These excursions are dependent on conditions at sea – extremely unpredictable in the winter months – but, on fair-weather days, boats tend to depart at regular intervals (times vary from charter to charter), irrespective of the number of passengers. For luxury boat trips – fully enclosed lounge, pub and aft-deck – visitors are urged to make prior reservations.

The tranquil waters of Table Bay come alive in summer with the not-to-be-missed **Dragon Boat Festival**.

Robben Island

One of the highlights of a day at the V&A Waterfront will almost surely be a cruise to **Robben Island**. But be warned that access to this World Heritage Site is restricted. Most boat trips do not include a tour of the island and it is unlikely that you will be allowed to disembark, unless you take an official tour.

Official tours are conducted exclusively by the **Robben Island Museum**. The 11.5-kilometre (7-mile) boat trip takes about half an hour each way, and the tour lasts about three hours. The fee includes a comprehensive tour of the political prison, and a bus ride that takes visitors to various sites across the island. Ferries bring visitors to the island's **Murray's Harbour**, named after 19th-century whaler John Murray.

This holding place of political prisoners during the days of apartheid has attracted enormous interest since the release of its most famous inmate, Nelson Mandela, in 1990. Today conservationists are trying to protect the delicate natural ecosystem and unique flora, and to preserve the 574-hectare (1 418-acre) island as a breeding place for seabirds. Since the beginning of 1997, Robben Island has been under the auspices of the Department of Arts and Culture. The prison has been converted into a museum commemorating the liberation struggle in South Africa against the apartheid government. Robben Island was declared a **World Heritage Site** in 1999, thus ensuring its protection and status as a symbol of freedom and triumph over oppression and discrimination. The history of Robben Island provides a fascinating look into the history of South Africa. Early explorers visited the small island to stock up on fresh provisions such as seal and penguin meat and eggs. It

sundowner, but one should not forget that the very existence of the docklands depended on majestic Table Bay. Once reserved almost exclusively for maritime trading and industry, Cape Town's revitalised harbour now plays host to a stream of passenger cruise liners and naval vessels paying courtesy visits. Table Bay also features prominently on the popular Cape Town Sailing Week as well as on the international sailing calendar. It remains an important stopover on one of the world's most prestigious yachting routes. The harbour is a major station on

was also a stopping point for ships, which collected mail left by sailors who passed this way.

A number of quarries are dotted across the island, and these played an important role in its history. There are stone and slate quarries, and two quarries of blue-stone on its beach, but the most renowned is 'Jan's Hole', the quarry from which Jan van Riebeeck collected Malmesbury slate to build parts of the Castle of Good Hope. Seashells from the island were also crushed and burned to make lime cement for the castle. More recently, the lime quarry was the place where political prisoners crushed the limestone used to maintain the island's roads.

Robben Island has served many purposes over the years. Originally, it was the holding 'pen' for livestock needed on the mainland, and went on to become a place of exile for mental patients. Between 1846 and 1931, the island was also a leper colony. The old leper morgue has been converted into offices, and the Lepers' Bath – once used by lepers who believed that the salt water would offer some relief for their sores – is today a tidal swimming pool. Visitors can see the separate leper settlements (men and women were housed apart) and both the cemetery and church alongside the site of the male leper colony. One of the most striking structures on the island is the **Church of the Good Shepherd**, designed by renowned architect Sir Herbert Baker, and built in 1895 for use by the male lepers.

Another highlight is the 18-metre (60-foot) **lighthouse**, erected in 1863, which is situated on Minto Hill – at 30 metres above sea level, the highest point on the island. Nearby is the Officers' Club and, just offshore, the wreck of *Fung Chung II*, a Taiwanese fishing vessel that foundered in 1977. The Officers' Club was once the island's abattoir and is built on Lady's Rock, named after Sister May Harvey, a nun who cared for the ailing lepers and who drowned here in the late 1800s. Not to be confused with the Officers' Club, the Club Building was built in the mid-1800s as the island home of the resident medical superintendent, and the cellars beneath the impressive Victorian structure still hold the chains with which 'troublesome' slaves were fettered.

An equally fine example of the architecture of the time is the **Guest House**, which was built in 1895 for the island's governor and the pastor, who occupied the lower level. Today, the Guest House is used as a venue for conferences.

In stark contrast to these colonial structures is the **kramat**, a Muslim shrine near the harbour and walls of the political prison. The kramat was built over the grave of Sayed Abduroman Moturu, the Prince of Madura, near Java, who died in exile on the island in 1754. For many prisoners, the kramat was a symbol of hope.

Robben Island is dotted with reminders of a more recent period of history, when the defence of Cape Town was monitored from the island during World War II. Outbuildings, bunkers and 9-inch guns may still be seen. **Varney's Fort** – the

OPPOSITE TOP *Political prisoner Robert Sobukwe of the Pan-Africanist Congress (PAC) was held separately from fellow inmates in a humble dwelling on the island.*

OPPOSITE MIDDLE *The entrance to the once infamous prison compound is the starting point for tours of the island.*

OPPOSITE BOTTOM *Tiny cell Number 5 still looks much as it did during Nelson Mandela's incarceration on the prison-island.*

ABOVE *Like the fishing boat which foundered here in 1977, many a vessel has met its end on Robben Island's treacherous reefs.*

first lime kiln to be built here – became a power station for the two powerful searchlights used during the war. Of particular note is the **Robben Island Primary School**, which was built in 1870 and used by World War II soldiers as a clubhouse. Other attractions include the **Garrison Church**, which still serves its original purpose, and the **Old Residency**, once home to local commissioners. The **John Craig Hall** was built during the war, and today serves as a venue for indoor sports and functions. Other modern facilities on the island include a post office, a small shop that serves as the local supermarket, a landing strip for aircraft, and an 18-hole mini golf course.

The natural heritage of Robben Island remains all-important. Today the fauna consists largely of steenbok, springbok and bontebok, and the birdlife includes a nesting colony of jackass penguins, as well as cormorants and even a few ostriches. The rapidly growing population of rabbits introduced to the island over the years has called for a culling programme to minimise the destruction of indigenous vegetation on which indigenous fauna depend for survival. The most renowned inhabitants, however, are the seals, after which the island is named – 'robben' is the Dutch word for seals. Because of the human activity of recent years, however, the seals have yet to re-establish a breeding colony here.

Most visitors come to see the island because of its political history, and the fact that it was, for a long period, home to many leaders of the liberation movement. The first prisoner held here was Autshumato, known in South African history books as 'Harry', who was banished here by Van Riebeeck. Another inmate was Makana, who was accused of stirring his Xhosa followers into an uprising against the British in 1819.

The Old Prison medium-security prison and the administration buildings of the Department of Correctional Services remain, as does the home of Pan-Africanist Congress leader Robert Sobukwe, who was held on the island by government

order, even after his sentence had expired. Built in 1963, the prison housed mostly political prisoners. It was only relieved of its sombre past in May 1991, when the remaining prisoners were either transferred or released. The most fascinating portion of the prison is **Nelson Mandela's cell**, which looks onto the courtyard of B-Section. Prior to his election as President of South Africa, Mr Mandela spent almost 19 years in Cell Number 5 until his transfer to Pollsmoor Prison in Tokai, and then to Victor Verster Prison outside Paarl, from where he was released on 11 February 1990.

OPPOSITE TOP *The restored Guest House was once the residence of the governor and pastor, but now plays host to conferences.*

OPPOSITE BOTTOM *Warning approaching vessels of impending danger, the island's lighthouse is still in working order.*

TOP *Robben Island's first black lighthouse keeper, Mr Jacobs, surveys the view from the top of the lighthouse.*

ABOVE *Many lepers, exiled to Robben Island for nearly a century, rest in the island cemetery.*

DAY
3

TABLE MOUNTAIN
& KIRSTENBOSCH

TABLE MOUNTAIN & KIRSTENBOSCH

Table Mountain • The Cableway • Walks and Trails • Lion's Head • Signal Hill
Devil's Peak • Kirstenbosch National Botanical Garden

For decades, the famed flat-topped mountain that forms the backdrop to the city of Cape Town – with Kirstenbosch National Botanical Garden on its eastern slopes – has enjoyed unparalleled status as the country's top tourist attraction. Today, both the mountain and the world-renowned gardens continue to attract more than two million visitors a year, second only to the V&A Waterfront on the docklands of Table Bay.

Flanked by Devil's Peak and Lion's Head, monolithic **Table Mountain** – which can be spotted from as far as 200 kilometres (124 miles) out at sea – was given its rather apt name by Portuguese explorer and adventurer Antonio de Saldanha. The impressive hulk of shale, sandstone and granite – Maclear's Beacon is the mountain's highest point – towers 1 086 metres (3 564 feet) above the city's shoreline, and its characteristic flat surface extends almost three kilometres, making it the country's most familiar landmark. When on occasion the front of the mountain is lit by floodlights at night, its imposing ramparts have an even more romantic quality.

The Cableway

Virtually every visitor to Cape Town's shores seems determined to venture to the summit of the mountain, and the old cableway, which has been in service since early last century, saw heavy traffic. For this reason, the Table Mountain Aerial Cableway Company renovated and upgraded the existing facilities in 1997 so that visitors may enjoy a faster and more efficient service.

The new cable car departs from the cable station at the top of Kloof Nek Road and takes five minutes to complete the trip to the summit. Visitors who do not have their own transport to the cable station may take a taxi or the bus, which leaves every 30 minutes from the Grand Parade bus depot. Queues can be expected during peak tourist season, but the wait to board the cable car is generally brief.

The cable car takes as many as 65 people at a time, and operates virtually throughout the year – depending, of course, on Cape Town's somewhat erratic weather conditions. The ascent is well worth any time spent in a queue, and the

---

PREVIOUS PAGES *The much-photographed flat-topped landmark that symbolises the Mother City, seen from Bloubergstrand.*

INSET *Rock hyrax, or dassies, may be seen cavorting among the rocks at the summit of Table Mountain.*

ABOVE *A chattering sugarbird pauses on one of Kirstenbosch's crane-like strelitzias.*

OPPOSITE *Dramatic lookout points atop Table Mountain afford exhilarating views of the city and its environs.*

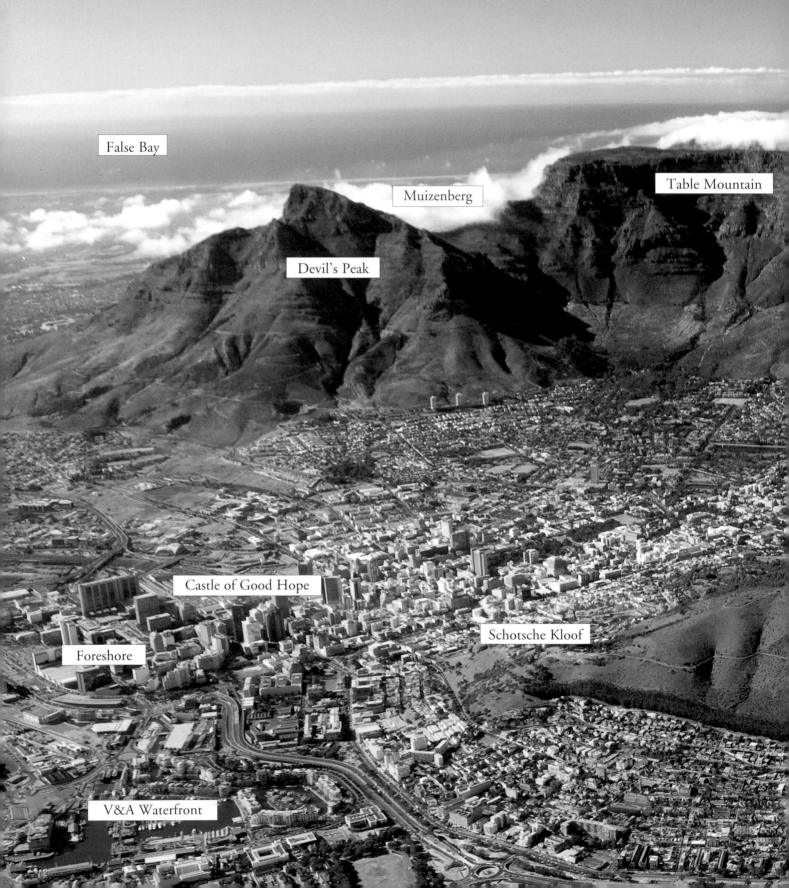

False Bay

Muizenberg

Table Mountain

Devil's Peak

Castle of Good Hope

Schotsche Kloof

Foreshore

V&A Waterfront

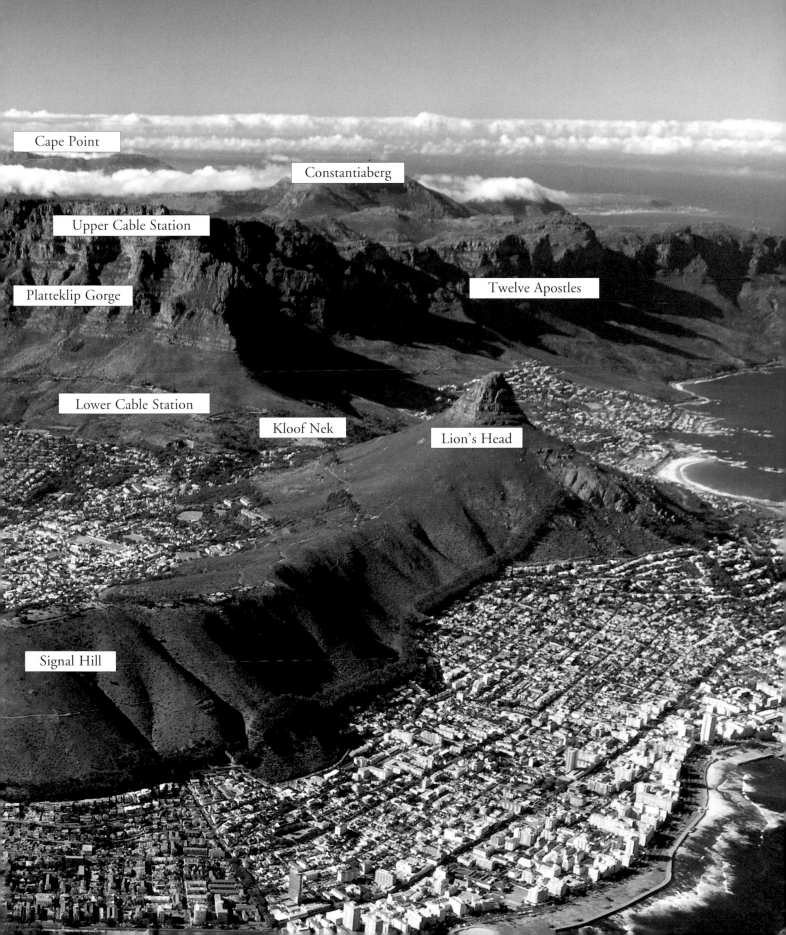

Cape Point

Constantiaberg

Upper Cable Station

Platteklip Gorge

Twelve Apostles

Lower Cable Station

Kloof Nek

Lion's Head

Signal Hill

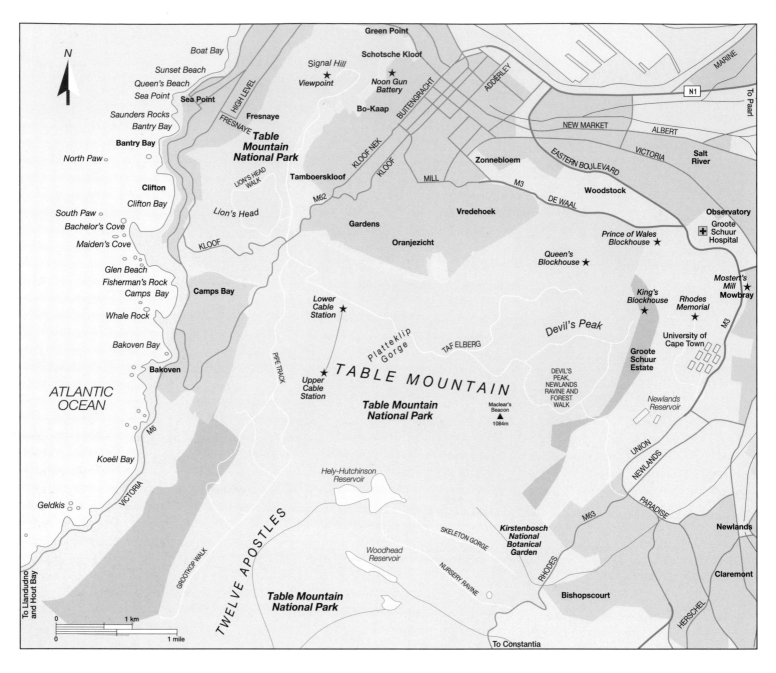

breathtaking view of the peninsula and surrounds from the summit is reward enough. Apart from the awesome panorama, perhaps the most impressive sight on Table Mountain is its unique array of flora and fauna.

Scurrying among the rocks and shrubs are rock hyrax – known locally as dassies – which have inhabited the mountain slopes since long before human settlement. These fascinating little creatures, with their shining black eyes and short-haired coats are, despite their rodent-like appearance, related to the elephant, and can be found on many of the high-lying, mountainous areas of the Cape.

Floral Fantasy

Table Mountain, with its spectacular assortment of vegetation, forms a vital part of the Cape Floral Kingdom, which includes more than 8 500 plants, flowers, trees and shrubs – comprising virtually all of the peninsula's indigenous floral heritage. The unique natural habitat of hardy, evergreen vegetation is known as fynbos (from the Afrikaans word meaning 'fine bush'),

and the peak flowering season sees nearly 1 500 plant species erupt in colour and texture. Floral gems include ericas, proteas – including the king protea, South Africa's national flower – and disas, the most familiar of which is the red *Disa uniflora*, also known as the Pride of Table Mountain, the provincial emblem of the Western Cape. A standout among tree species is the majestic silver tree, with its distinctive silver-grey foliage.

A World Apart

For those visitors who may have chosen to walk up the slopes and are in need of sustenance, the summit boasts the Table Mountain Café, which offers light lunches and other refreshments. The Shop on the Top stocks souvenirs and mementoes, including postcards and books, as well as essentials such as sunscreen and disposable cameras. Visitors may also post a letter that will bear the prized postmark indicating that it was posted from the top of Table Mountain. A relief model of the peninsula pinpoints landmarks and provides a useful point for orientation. The Cableway company also offers conference facilities that take in the views from the Old Stone Balcony, the Bistro and the Twelve Apostles Terrace.

PREVIOUS PAGES *Majestic Table Mountain forms part of a chain of mountains reaching southward to distant Cape Point.*

OPPOSITE *Captured in a scale model situated at the top of the mountain, the peninsula invites visitors to explore its treasures.*

ABOVE *A network of gentle footpaths guides walkers to view-sites and points of interest around the summit of Table Mountain.*

Walking the Mountain

With a spectacular view across the **Twelve Apostles** – there are, in fact, 17 peaks in this range – to Cape Point, the mountain is popular with both serious hikers and casual amblers. The latter may prefer to stroll along the Tortoise, Rock Dassie or Klipspringer walks – short, demarcated summit trails that range in duration from five to 30 minutes. Climbers should always be accompanied by either a group of companions or a recognised guide. All too often, climbers have either lost their way or fallen victim to the mountain's many cliffs and precipices. Should you wish to arrange an organised venture into the rocky terrain, contact the **Mountain Club of South Africa**, which can provide details about guides.

Table Mountain boasts about 300 different walks, which vary in distance and demand various degrees of both stamina and fitness. Apart from a guide, climbers should also wear suitable climbing shoes or boots, plan for both extremes of weather, pack enough food, water and emergency supplies and, most importantly, stick to the assigned footpaths. Officials also recommend that climbers take along a cellular telephone if possible, and let friends or family members know where they will be walking and when they expect to return.

Climbing the Mountain

A number of maps detail most of the walking and climbing routes on the mountain, and may prove handy – if not necessary – to climbers. Maps are available from the shop at the top of the mountain, and outlets such as those at Kirstenbosch National Botanical Garden and other city souvenir shops.

The **Platteklip Gorge** walk on the Kloof Nek side of the mountain extends between the two cableway stations, and is a hike up the mountain which should take about 2.5 hours to

complete. The **Contour Path** follows the contour line from majestic **Rhodes Memorial** directly to Kirstenbosch, taking about two to three hours to complete. From Kirstenbosch, hikers may walk to both Cecilia Ravine and Cecilia Forest in the suburb of Newlands. An alternative route is the circular walk from the front of the mountain to the **Woodhead** and **Hely-Hutchinson** dams and the **Waterworks Museum**, which houses the history of the two reservoirs. Yet another choice may be to walk up **Nursery Ravine** from Kirstenbosch to the Woodhead Dam, and then down Cecilia Ravine. Exploring Table Mountain is a popular pastime for locals as well as visitors, and a number of hiking and travel guides focus on the mountain's walks and trails.

Lion's Head

To the west of Table Mountain rears **Lion's Head**, from the base of which extends Signal Hill. For keen climbers, Lion's Head provides something of a challenge and casual hikers should note that it is not all level ground and pleasant strolling. Metal ladders and chains have been inserted into the rock face to assist climbers to reach the top of the 669-metre (2 195-foot) peak. Although not gruelling, the climb requires some degree of effort. A pleasant alternative, however, is to drive along Signal Hill. The brightly painted **kramat** visible from the road is one of many shrines dotted around the Cape Peninsula to honour Islamic leaders, buried there. Members of the Cape's large Muslim community believe that these shrines watch over and protect the citizens of Cape Town. Visitors are welcome, but are reminded that dress should be appropriate to the holy ground, and that it is polite to leave your shoes at the door.

Signal Hill

Signal Hill, the mountainous knoll that divides the city from Sea Point and beyond, looks across exclusive residential suburbs such as Bantry Bay and a spectacular strip of white beaches. At the end of the summit drive is a parking area, viewing point and picnic facilities. Of course, Signal Hill is famous not only as one of the best vantage points from which to watch the sunset, but also as the site of the **noon gun**. This old naval cannon is fired every day of the week (except Sundays) from a battery on Schotsche Kloof just below the summit of Signal Hill, and the sound reverberates throughout the City Bowl. Formerly fired from the grounds of the Castle of Good Hope,

---

TOP LEFT *The rotating floor of the cable car affords visitors a 360-degree view of the mountain slopes and the city below.*

TOP RIGHT *The kramat on Signal Hill is a shrine to the Muslim missionary, Sheikh Mohamed Hassen Ghaibie Shah.*

ABOVE *The echoing boom of the noon gun has signalled midday since the earliest days of the settlement.*

OPPOSITE TOP *Wisps of the cloud so aptly named The Table Cloth drift past the bulk of Lion's Head.*

OPPOSITE BOTTOM *On a clear day, paragliders relish the thrill of a bird's-eye view of the mountain and city below.*

the noon gun signals midday, but also serves as a reminder of those who lost their lives during the two world wars. In days gone by, flags were also raised here so that the town could get ready for the arrival of ships in Table Bay.

Devil's Peak

On the slopes of Devil's Peak, on the eastern side of Table Mountain, are three blockhouses that were built by British troops during the second British occupation of the Cape (1806). The **Queen's Blockhouse** still stands and has been faithfully restored, but only rubble remains of the **Prince of Wales Blockhouse**. Of the three, the most impressive is the **King's Blockhouse**, formerly a prison and today a historical monument. There is little else on the slopes of Devil's Peak, yet the 1 002-metre (3 288-foot) peak remains a popular hiking destination. It should, however, be tackled only by experienced climbers and, even then, in the company of a guide familiar with the mountain trails.

Kirstenbosch

The **Kirstenbosch National Botanical Garden** is run by the National Biodiversity Institute, and the information office at the main entrance provides a wealth of material on the present, past and future of this imposing wonderland, known throughout

the world for its spectacular beauty and incredible diversity of plants. Known informally as Kirstenbosch, the lush gardens spread across Table Mountain's eastern slopes and extend up to Maclear's Beacon. There is ample free parking and bus services run to and from the railway stations at Mowbray and nearby Claremont. There is an entrance fee.

The People's Garden

On his death in 1902, Cecil John Rhodes – whose memorial stands on the lower slopes of Devil's Peak – left the grounds of Kirstenbosch to the South African people, and the gardens were formally established in 1913. Today, Kirstenbosch comprises over 500 hectares (1 235 acres), as well as 478 hectares (1 181 acres) of fynbos and natural forest. The landscape includes nearly 7 000 species of indigenous plants, nearly 1 000 of which occur naturally within the area – many are unique to the slopes of Table Mountain. Some 36 hectares (89 acres) are reserved solely for cultivation and research.

The Compton Herbarium

Originally situated within the perimeter of the gardens, the **Compton Herbarium** was recently moved to nearly five hectares (12 acres) of ground bought from the City of Cape

Scientists and educators have also established the Goldfields Environmental Education Centre. The centre provides outings for school groups and other interested parties, and holds lectures on the wildlife of southern Africa.

Birdsong

As may be expected in such a natural wonderland, the birdlife is prolific. The information office stocks checklists of those species that may be spotted within the confines of the gardens, and Colin Paterson-Jones's *Visitor's Guide to Kirstenbosch* (Random House Struik, 2004) may prove essential reading on both the wildlife and the story of these beautiful gardens. This handy book is available from The Garden Shop at the main gate, which also stocks books on the country, small gifts and mementoes, and a wide selection of indigenous plants.

The Attractions

An added attraction of the gardens is the popular **summertime concerts**. Flocks of music lovers congregate on the lawns on Sunday evenings to enjoy an eclectic repertoire ranging from classical and choral music to the vibrant sounds of local bands.

In 1998, Kirstenbosch opened a **visitors' centre**, located near the main entrance off Rhodes Drive. The complex provides access to the impressive stone and glass **conservatory** aptly known as the Glass House. The conservatory displays arid-adapted and alpine species that require specific moisture and temperature conditions and so cannot be displayed out of doors. The centrepiece of the facility is a large baobab tree that was brought to Kirstenbosch from Limpopo province. Other attractions include the Kirstenbosch Garden Centre, Visitors' Centre Shop, a landscape centre and a bookshop. Restaurants include the famed Silvertree Restaurant and Fynbos Deli, as well as Caffe Botanica and the ever-popular Kirstenbosch Tea Room.

The **Kirstenbosch Craft Market**, held on the last Sunday of every month (except in winter), is a meeting place for fine crafters from across the peninsula, who offer a dizzying array of goods ranging from traditional sculptures, beadwork and weaving to ceramics, jewellery and clothing. All the goods are of a very high quality, as the Botanical Society keeps a tight control.

Town. The herbarium was named in 1919 for RH Compton, the then director of the National Botanical Garden, under whose auspices the *Journal of South African Botany* would eventually be launched in 1935. The facility has now extended its original function to include a research centre and laboratory dealing largely with the scientific aspects of the country's extensive plant life. Today, the research centre – which is closed to the public – houses nearly half a million botanical specimens, and its botanists work with colleagues throughout the world in order to study and protect the natural heritage of the region.

Top Left *Among the fynbos species of the Cape Floral Kingdom that are found in Kirstenbosch are ericas, pictured here.*

Middle left *The delicate blooms of the pincushion protea may vary from soft yellow to dusky pink.*

Bottom Left *Robust and strong, the majestic king protea represents one of the garden's most prolific plant species.*

Opposite *With its burst of colour and glorious backdrop, Kirstenbosch is one of the world's most beautiful botanical gardens.*

Table Mountain National Park

Kirstenbosch forms part of the greater Table Mountain National Park, which was declared a World Heritage Site in 2004. The national park spans Lion's Head to Devil's Peak, taking in the sweeping escarpment of the Twelve Apostles, the jagged splendour of Chapman's Peak and weaves along Ou Kaapseweg before descending towards Cape Point. The park includes within its official boundaries many reserves and sanctuaries that were scattered across the peninsula, including the Cape of Good Hope Nature Reserve.

Walks through Kirstenbosch

Many visitors to Kirstenbosch are keen to traverse the mountain landscape, and several trails lead up the mountain slopes from the gardens. As with any walk or climb through unfamiliar territory, visitors are urged to take precautions and to plan their walk with the aid of maps and guides. The many reliable footpaths offer dramatic views and provide ideal routes, and should be adhered to at all times. Should you require a guide, enquire at the main gate, and expect to pay a small fee for the assurance of personal safety.

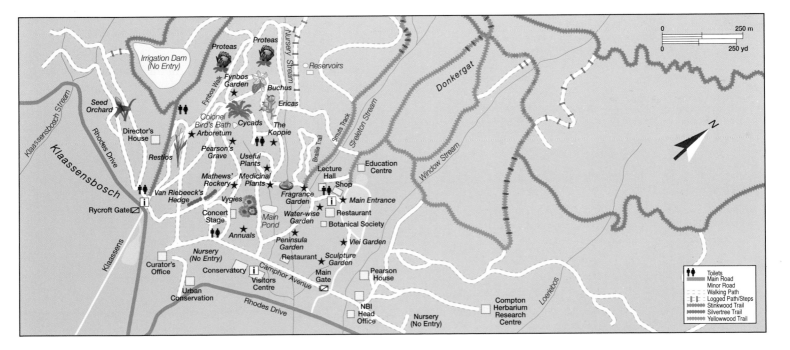

Table Mountain & Kirstenbosch

The Dell and Cycad Amphitheatre

Nestled in the Dell below the famed Cycad Amphitheatre is a bird-shaped well fed throughout the year by the springs that flow into it. Edged with stones brought to the Cape from Batavia, the pool is known – albeit mistakenly – as Lady Anne Barnard's Bath, in reference to the wife of Andrew Barnard, the secretary to the governor, Earl Macartney. Lady Anne acted as First Lady and official hostess during her stay at the Cape. The bath itself is, in fact, called **Colonel Bird's Bath**, after Colonel Christopher Bird, the civil servant who built it in about 1811 – some years after Lady Anne left the shores of the Cape!

The area surrounding the bath boasts not only all four of the country's indigenous yellowwood tree species, but also the only Cape species of holly *Ilex mitis*, and, of course, the **Cycad Amphitheatre**. These non-flowering, seed-bearing plants, ranged up the steep slope, belong to an ancient order of plants that flourished many millions of years ago. Although cycads bear some resemblance to palm trees, they are in fact unrelated. Cycads were among the first species planted in the newly established Kirstenbosch by the garden's first director, Professor Harold Pearson, in 1903. Pearson's grave, alongside the collection of cycads, is watched over by an enormous blue Atlas cedar shipped from Kew Gardens in London.

Mathews' Rockery

A collection of mostly succulents from southern Africa's arid regions, the **Mathews' Rockery** was initiated by the garden's first curator, JW Mathews, who began putting together the sandstone rockery in 1927. In addition to the sometimes bizarre shapes of the succulents, the garden also boasts an assortment of bulb flowers and other plants, such as aloes, which erupt in colour during the winter months. From the path leading to both the rockery and the Dell, visitors may still see portions of Jan van Riebeeck's **wild almond hedge**, which marked the boundary of the very first European settlement at the Cape.

Pelargonium Koppie and Environs

Home to the colourful pelargoniums, **Pelargonium Koppie** abounds with dry fynbos species. Along the footpath through the area is also the aromatic **herb garden**, a popular stopping point at which to see the rooibos and honey tea bushes – often used to brew herbal tea – that grow here. All the plants' parts are combined to create fragrant perfumes, food flavouring and home medicines.

A fascinating diversion for the visitor is the aptly named **Fragrance Garden** opposite the herb garden. While the plants display interesting hues of grey, blue and green, the air here is thick with the aroma of scented leaves, which almost beg to be touched, felt and smelled. The informative signs are printed in large type, with Braille provided for the benefit of sight-impaired visitors. The information provided is both interesting and informative, and invites the reader to follow the half-kilometre **Braille Trail** nearby. A rope guides visitors to the approximately 10 stopping points at which further descriptions and details are provided in Braille and print.

Above *With more than 500 hectares (1 235 acres) of verdant terrain, Kirstenbosch offers many corners of solitary beauty.*

Opposite Top *The intoxicating scents of the Fragrance Garden are an endless delight to children and adults alike.*

Opposite Bottom *The summer sunset concerts held on Sundays at Kirstenbosch are popular with visitors and locals.*

The Camphor Avenue

The noble camphor trees that line this avenue were introduced by the Cape premier and businessman Cecil John Rhodes when the avenue still served as part of the main road between Newlands and Hout Bay.

The area surrounding this exotic avenue of trees boasts an array of cycads and vibrantly coloured flowers, while the conservatory lies directly opposite.

Fynbos

The paved **Fynbos Walk** extends from Rycroft Gate to Pelargonium Koppie, along the higher slopes of Kirstenbosch's cultivated section. Near the gate are gardens devoted to the three most prominent fynbos groups – restio, protea and erica. Among the botanical curiosities to be found in the restio garden are reeds that are said to live for up to 60 years, while the erica garden is a constant parade of colour as the 600 different

USEFUL INFORMATION

Caffe Botanica: Kirstenbosch; tel: 021 762-6841
Cape Town Tourism: V&A Waterfront Gateway Information Office; tel: 021 405 4500; Cape Town Routes Unlimited; tel: 021 487 4800; www.tourismcapetown.co.za
Kirstenbosch Information Office: Open 8am–7pm daily; tel: 021 799-8783
Kirstenbosch National Botanical Garden: Rhodes Dr., Newlands; open 8am–7pm daily; tel: 021 799-8899; www.sanbi.org
Kirstenbosch Tea Room: Open 9am–5pm daily; tel: 021 797-4883
Mountain Club of South Africa: 97 Hatfield St, Gardens; tel: 021 465-3412
Silvertree Restaurant: Kirstenbosch; tel: 021 762-9585
South African National Biodiversity Institute: Open 8am–7pm daily; tel: 021 797-2090
Table Mountain Aerial Cableway Company: tel: 021 424-8181 Depart from lower cable station on Tafelberg Rd (off Kloof Nek Rd). Prices vary according to season. Open year round, but may be limited by wind conditions at the summit.
The Garden Shop: Open 8am–7pm daily; tel: 021 797-1305
The Glass House: Open 11am–4pm daily; tel: 021 799-8737

species bloom throughout the year. The protea garden, with its subdued shades, is at its best in late March and early April, while the garden's leucadendrons and silver trees – the 6-kilometre (3.7-mile) forest trail shows these at their finest – bloom in spring. Summer is the turn of the pincushions.

DAY 4

THE ATLANTIC
SEABOARD

The Atlantic Seaboard

Green Point • Mouille Point • Three Anchor Bay & Sea Point • Bantry Bay • Clifton • Camps Bay
Bakoven • Llandudno • Sandy Bay • Suikerbossie • Hout Bay • Chapman's Peak Drive • Noordhoek

The strip of the peninsula's shoreline commonly known as the Atlantic seaboard stretches some 55 kilometres (34 miles) from the waters of Table Bay along the western coast to the nature reserve at Cape Point. The exceptional beaches and rugged mountains along this coastline not only make this a popular drive – for both locals and visitors – but also provide outstanding views across the Atlantic Ocean, with some of the most spectacular sunsets in the world. Naturally, the plush homes along this coast sell for millions.

Green Point

On the slopes above the V&A Waterfront and Table Bay is the seaside suburb of **Green Point**. Along with Sea Point, Green Point became home to well-heeled segments of Cape society in the 1940s and 1950s. With the development of the seafront, many of the area's numerous apartment blocks are in demand once again as South Africans and wealthy foreign investors clamour for the sea views. As expected, the few hotels and residential developments here are equally exclusive.

Visitors leaving the Waterfront from the Green Point exit will immediately encounter a majestic old building resembling a fort. This is the century-old Somerset Hospital, focal point of a multimillion-rand redevelopment programme adjoining the Waterfront and the international-standard stadium at Green Point. The old buildings have seen extensive renovation that has converted the precinct to an important medical facility that includes an emergency trauma unit originally designed to facilitate medical requirements for the 2010 soccer World Cup, laboratory services, a community health centre and medical staff accommodation.

Alongside Somerset Hospital stretch the grassy fairways of Green Point's Metropolitan Golf Course, and behind is **Cape Town Stadium**. Part of both the golf course and the Green Point Common have been given over to the new hi-tech stadium, the nerve centre of the city's hosting of the soccer World Cup in 2010. The old Green Point Stadium on this site was one of Cape Town's oldest and welcomed many international performers to its stage. The brand-new

PREVIOUS PAGES *With the Atlantic at its calmest, the last rays of the setting sun cast a warm glow over Sea Point.*

INSET *Glorious sunny summer days make the palm-fringed beach at Camps Bay the place to see and be seen.*

ABOVE *With a laid-back vibe reminiscent of Los Angeles, the Sea Point Promenade is popular with both joggers and walkers.*

OPPOSITE *Its four pristine beaches have earned Clifton an international reputation as the Cape's premier beach spot.*

Table Mountain

Reservoirs

Twelve Apostles

Bakoven

Hout Bay ➡

stadium that now takes pride of place here was erected during the run-up to the World Cup, and is now one of the finest in southern Africa. It boasts a state-of-the-art retractable roof as well as top-of-the range function facilities. It also has seating capacity for some 50 000 spectators, following the disassembly of approximately 18 000 seats after the World Cup to make standing room for other high-profile events beyond the spectator sports generally hosted here. Apart from ball sports, the new world-class stadium also hosts other major events. For a calendar of events be sure to visit the impressive new Visitors' Centre at the heart of the complex.

Mouille Point

A tiny area to the west of the V&A Waterfront, and enclosed by the suburb of Green Point, **Mouille Point** is most noted for its wide vista of open ocean and its conspicuous lighthouse. Erected by Herman Schutte as long ago as 1824, the **Green Point Lighthouse** – named after the surrounding suburb rather than its precise location – is the oldest of its kind in the country. The light that once warned ships of the rocky coastline

originally emanated from a simple oil lantern. This was not particularly reliable on misty Cape evenings, but the modern device – of 850 000 candlepower – can be seen nearly 25 kilometres (15 miles) out to sea. Alongside the distinctive red-and-white striped structure is a small pleasure park for children, including a miniature golf course, train rides and an ice-cream stand. Virtually next door to the lighthouse is the children's play centre and the delightful **Serendipity Maze,** a series of hedged-in passageways that eventually lead to the centre.

Three Anchor Bay and Sea Point

On the seaward side of Signal Hill lie Three Anchor Bay and Sea Point, and the coastal stretch of Beach Road. The suburb of **Sea Point**, with its profusion of once-plush hotels and highrise accommodation, is one of the continent's most populated areas, and was once the playground of the rich and famous. Although property prices are still relatively high, Sea Point saw a dip in popularity in the late 1990s when focus shifted to the developing V&A Waterfront and it became considerably less sought-after as a residential area as a result. However, since the boost in both local and international interest in Cape Town in the first years of the new millennium, matters have changed somewhat. With the soaring property prices and the scramble for sea views and beachfront accommodation, Sea Point is rapidly regaining popularity, especially among investors clamouring for real estate along the Atlantic seaboard. Even sadly neglected apartments and beach bungalows are being snapped up and renovated, either as plush new coastal retreats for the wealthy or as rental accommodation available – at rather high prices – to the holidaymakers who flock here during the 'In Season'. Today, Sea Point is once again a hubbub of entertainment, boasting a lively strip of trendy nightclubs, all-night cafés, bistros and restaurants, notably **Harveys at The Mansions**, the signature restaurant of the landmark **Winchester Mansions** on Beach Road, where the executive chef creates some of the finest Mediterranean fare in Cape Town.

Sun-worshippers of all shapes and sizes tend to congregate along the 3 kilometres (2 miles) of the **Sea Point Promenade**, popular among casual strollers, joggers, young skateboarders

PREVIOUS PAGES *Cape Town's Atlantic coast embraces a clutch of plush residential enclaves, backed by the lofty Twelve Apostles.*

LEFT *Despite the warning provided by the historic Green Point Lighthouse, many vessels have foundered on the rocky shore.*

OPPOSITE TOP *Blessed with breathtaking views, The Bay Hotel in Camps Bay is a haven of luxury.*

OPPOSITE BOTTOM *Camps Bay's long stretch of fine beach is the playground of bronzed volleyballers and sun-worshippers.*

and rollerbladers. The promenade has seen a number of facelifts over the years, but it is still the breathtaking panorama over the ocean that is its most significant attraction, the expanse of Atlantic Ocean dotted with surfers braving the notoriously icy waters. The beaches below tend to be a little crowded over the summer months and parking is at a premium, but these are minor discomforts considering the magnificent setting.

The Leisure Strip

Southwest along the coast from Sea Point lies the band of upmarket residential properties unofficially known as **Millionaires' Mile**. Stretching along winding Victoria Road from Bantry Bay through Clifton, Camps Bay and Bakoven to distant Llandudno, this strip is considerably longer than a mile, but it is clearly the playground of the wealthy. The wind-free, sun-blessed beaches provide an idyllic setting in which to relax – and the palatial homes along this coast are understandably expensive.

Beyond **Bantry Bay**, which nestles along the western slopes of Signal Hill and Lion's Head, lies **Clifton**, with its four immaculate beaches. Simply named First, Second, Third and Fourth, the Clifton beaches are famed the world over for their consummate splendour. The beaches are separated by granite outcrops that also act as a shelter from the southeasterly wind that plagues many of the Cape's less-favoured sunspots. Clifton is ideal for sunbathing and, in summer (December to February), the white sands are usually draped with scantily-clad bodies soaking up the Cape sun. First Beach is renowned for its sun-worshipping trendy set, while Third is a favourite of the teens, and Fourth Beach, with its nearby parking and refreshment facilities, caters mostly for family outings. The sun drenches these relatively secluded stretches virtually from

sunrise to sunset, and revellers often party on into the night with picnic suppers. So, if you're prepared to fight it out with the residents, hundreds of locals and other fun-seekers for the limited parking space, Clifton's beaches are the place to be if you want to experience the very best the Cape has to offer.

Luxury Living

Equally exclusive is **Camps Bay**, which lies at the foot of the Twelve Apostles – the mountain rampart that constitutes the western front of Table Mountain. Hedged in by granite boulders at each extreme, the enclave that is Camps Bay embraces a palm-fringed expanse of pristine white sand that looks as if it has come straight out of a Caribbean holiday brochure. Known in the late 1700s as Die Baay van Von Kamptz, after Frederick von Kamptz, the owner of the original farm, Ravenstyn, Camps Bay is a lively, stylish place: paragliders touch down dramatically on sands that play host to an exciting annual beach volleyball season, and holidaymakers picnic on the grassy margins, while children cavort in the tidal pools. There is even a bowling green for the less adventurous. But, because Camps Bay is not as sheltered as Clifton, the wind can be an annoyance and the sea volatile at times.

The landward side of Victoria Road is lined with shops, bistros – many with shaded pavement tables – and hotels. Overlooking the beach is the well-appointed, five-star **Bay Hotel**, boasting the sophisticated Rotunda ballroom. **Blues** restaurant offers equally impressive vistas over Camps Bay Beach.

For a taste of the lively arts, take in one of the current shows – mostly comedy, farce and light musical productions – at the **Theatre on the Bay**, a landmark theatre that features scrolled drapery over its distinctive facade. The privately owned theatre has become a reliable showcase for local theatre, and nights out here often end with after-theatre dinner or sundowners at one of the vibey eateries that line Victoria Road, including ever-popular Blues, Paranga (at The Promenade), Summerville, Tuscany Beach and Theo's. Sundowners are best enjoyed, though, from the trendy balconies of **Baraza** and **The Grand.**

If the day has proved demanding, both Kloof Road and Camps Bay Drive will take weary travellers back over Lion's Head right into the City Bowl. But, for the more spritely, the remainder of the drive around the peninsula may prove to be the most exciting.

Bakoven to Llandudno

Just beyond stylish Camps Bay is a small, rather isolated little beach. Lying on Bakoven Bay, tiny **Bakoven Beach** is not ideal

---

ABOVE *Carved mementoes and other crafts are offered for sale along the panoramic route between Bakoven and Llandudno.*

OPPOSITE *With many stretches of protected sand, Cape beaches are perfect for the young and the young at heart.*

for swimming or watersports – thick beds of seaweed and kelp clog the water – but is ideal for soaking up the sun. Unlike the more popular beaches, it does not cater for crowds so there are hardly any shops or cafés nearby. To reach this pebbly hideaway, you will have to brave the pathway down from the parking lot.

The road from Bakoven to Llandudno and beyond is a popular scenic drive. Just outside Bakoven, there is a substantial roadside market peppered with stalls selling curios such as seashells, carvings, biltong and indigenous crafts. About halfway between Camps Bay and Llandudno lie a braai and picnic area with rockpools and a string of beaches popular with divers who swim out to the shipwreck off the coast.

The luxurious **Twelve Apostles Hotel**, surrounded by the fynbos that spreads across the slopes of the mountain range, is a five-star establishment that boasts 70 elegant rooms and suites, each linked by walkways that offer splendid views across the ocean below.

Despite the fact that the water of the Atlantic tends to be very cold, and swimming can be uncomfortable, the beaches along the Atlantic seaboard are perennially popular, and property prices are steep. Nowhere is this clearer than in the sought-after residential enclave of **Llandudno**, where luxury homes line the slopes that lead steeply down to a fine sandy beach. Once again, massive granite boulders shelter Llandudno's beach and residential area. The mood here is laid-back and slow, and perfect for relaxing on a hot day. The placid waters are deceptive, however, and have claimed their fair share of victims. The tanker *Romelia* came to grief off Sunset Rocks in 1977 while under tow, and the wreck may still be seen at low tide.

Further along is **Sandy Bay**, perhaps one of the Cape's most famous beaches and Cape Town's unofficial nudist hangout. Access is via Victoria and Llandudno roads. The latter winds into Fishermen's Bend, and bathers should turn right into Oakburn Road and then left into Leeukoppie – the home of hotel magnate Sol Kerzner (of Sun City and Lost City fame) looks loftily from above – and into the carpark at Sunset Rocks.

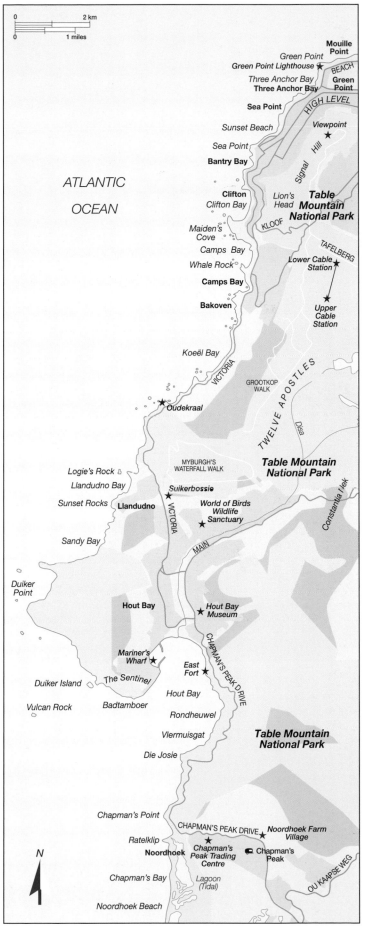

Because Sandy Bay is secluded, visitors will need to follow the footpath for about 15 to 20 minutes in order to reach the beach, which is surrounded by rocks and virtually impenetrable fynbos, making it ideal for bathing *au naturel*. Sadly, the natural splendour of Sandy Bay is also threatened by development, but bathers may still enjoy a day under the African sun.

Perched on the slopes of Klein Leeukoppie, just a few kilometres from Llandudno along Victoria Road, is **Suikerbossie**. This celebrated tearoom and restaurant serves an outstanding menu, and kosher meals are also readily available. This delightful stopover is an immensely popular venue for both afternoon tea and lunch – in fact, be sure to book if visiting on a Sunday – and offers magnificent views across the waters of Hout Bay.

Hout Bay

Because of its relative seclusion and the staunch 'patriotism' of its 'citizens', the fishing village of **Hout Bay** has unofficially become known as the Republic of Hout Bay, and realistic passports may even be purchased from enthusiastic custodians. Visitors may reach Hout Bay either from Victoria Road and Suikerbossie, or from the southern suburbs via Main Road. Buses depart at 20-minute intervals from the main bus terminus at the revamped Cape Town railway station with the first bus departing at 5.30am and the last departing at 5.30pm.

Despite rapid expansion in recent years, the fishing village that is Hout Bay remains relatively unscathed by modern development, and maintains a decidedly rural atmosphere. As a centre for many home-based industries, artists and craft traders, the village remains true to its harbour origins. Its name comes from the Dutch (and Afrikaans) word for timber, for the valley was a source of wood during the early days of the Cape colony. Hout Bay is still an important fishing harbour, and is renowned throughout the country for its fresh fish and seafood – be sure to make a stop at **Snoekies**, the city's favourite fresh fish market. Crayfish and other seafood delicacies are exported directly from the docks, and a **Snoek Derby** and a **Seafood Festival** are held annually. Throughout the year, and especially during the annual **Hout Bay Harbour Festival** in August, enthusiastic crowds gather at the harbour, crowded with boats of every description, and at the **Mariner's Wharf** complex, with its outstanding seafood restaurant, fish markets and curio shops. An exciting alternative to the standard shopping experience is to buy an oyster from the

Pearl Factory, and open it to find out whether your investment paid off in the form of a perfect pearl.

Pleasure seekers will be thrilled to find that Hout Bay offers many diversions: the long, curving beach provides safe and enjoyable swimming; small sailboats are available for hire; and there are a number of cruise operators in the area. **Circe Launches** offers sundowner cruises to the V&A Waterfront, Duiker Island (seabirds and seals) and Seal Island, while **Hooked-on-Africa** offers fishing tours.

OPPOSITE TOP *Local fishermen offer their fresh fare at Hout Bay's old harbour.*

OPPOSITE MIDDLE *Hout Bay is a haven for the peninsula's many craftspeople – and for curio-buying visitors.*

OPPOSITE BOTTOM *With the atmosphere of a fishing village, Mariner's Wharf is an emporium of seaside delights.*

ABOVE *From across Hout Bay, the bold silhouette of The Sentinel, on the right, marks the entrance to the bay.*

RIGHT *Competing with over 400 species at the World of Birds, the scarlet ibis boasts perhaps the most arresting plumage.*

The character and ambience of the village are accurately captured in the hushed drum of trading during the regular pavement flea market. Hout Bay's Main Road is much like that of any small hamlet, with a spattering of craft and clothing shops, banking and commercial activity, and steakhouses and other eateries. One of the most remarkable buildings, however, is **Kronendal**. This Cape Dutch home was built at the turn of the 18th century by a Johannes van Helsdingen and is Cape Town's only surviving example of the typical H-plan buildings of the period. Having been a tearoom, suite of offices and an antique dealership, **Kronendal** now houses the Kitima restaurant. The popular **Lookout Deck**, right on the waterfront, is one of the most frequented sundowner spots on the local scene, while **Dunes**, a lively restaurant and local watering hole, also has its faithful regulars, as well as plenty of visitors who are drawn to its relaxed and warm atmosphere virtually on the water's edge.

For a peek into the absorbing history of the Hout Bay area and to enquire about one of the many walks and trails among the unspoilt terrain of the area, go directly to the **Hout Bay Museum** on St Andrews Road.

Chapman's Peak Drive

At the start of the Cape's most spectacular and most scenic drive stands the **Chapman's Peak Hotel**. Its expansive, shady verandah hosts a popular eatery and bar in the summer months – the cosy interior is ideal in winter – and serves some of the finest seafood available on the peninsula. Visitors may also notice the bronze statue of a leopard atop the rocks close to the shore. This statue commemorates the Cape leopard, the last surviving of which was killed in Hout Bay, an area once teeming with wildlife.

Magnificent **Chapman's Peak Drive** – excavated from the mountain face at the boundary between the soft sandstone and hard granite layers and opened in 1922 – winds precariously for approximately 10 kilometres (6 miles) from Hout Bay to Noordhoek. For many years since, disastrous rockfalls have claimed the lives of many passing motorists. In 2000, following a spate of rockfalls, the route was closed. What ensued were three years of massive repairs, which irrevocably changed the face of the mountain but ultimately made it safer to enjoy. Today, the winding route, a toll road that continues to close intermittently during the rainy season, represents the most visually spectacular – as well as the most physically demanding – segment of both The Cape Argus Pick n Pay Cycle Tour (March) and the Two Oceans Marathon (April).

Nature lovers must visit the **World of Birds** on Valley Road. Initiated by well-known local resident Walter Mangold as a rescue station for sick or wounded birds, World of Birds is home to more than 450 indigenous species, housed in spacious aviaries. Bird enthusiasts and casual visitors can walk through the carefully designed habitats within the cages. Highlights among the facility's more than 3 000 residents include the squirrel monkeys, meerkats, colourful, chattering macaws, majestic blue cranes, penguins and a collection of formidable-looking owls.

The peak itself is about 600 metres (1 970 feet) high and, naturally, affords unsurpassed views over the ocean below. The multitude of roadside vantage points allow visitors the opportunity to take in one of the peninsula's most magnificent sights, and the sunsets here are particularly breathtaking. The road is narrow, so motorists should always exercise caution on this route. To the north, the sheer cliffs of The Sentinel loom over the entrance to Hout Bay. To the south lies Noordhoek and the scenic route to Cape Point.

Noordhoek

Noordhoek is perhaps most renowned for its pristine beach and unsullied environment, and so is the favoured homeground of Capetonians who wish to escape the frenzied city life in favour of the rural tranquillity of farms and smallholdings. Many artists live here, and the local galleries and craft shops provide much to tempt art lovers. The sparkling beach on the west end of Noordhoek Valley covers about 8 kilometres (5 miles) of coastline from the foot of Chapman's Peak to the fishing village of Kommetjie on Chapman's Bay. Although it is well suited to sunbathing or a leisurely seaside stroll, the waters here can be rather dangerous, so swimmers are urged to play it safe and take the necessary precautions for safe bathing.

Longbeach Mall – a grand shopping complex – is a recent addition to the valley. The people of Noordhoek – relatively isolated from the city life over the mountain – so treasure

the rural atmosphere that it was only in 2001 that such a modern convenience has been allowed to spring up in their midst.

Nearby is the Red Herring restaurant and pub, an old favourite that has become something of a legend in these parts and especially well known for its live music evenings held over weekends. Further along the main road toward Fish Hoek and Kommetjie lies **Noordhoek Farm Village**, a charming collection of whitewashed buildings that shelter craft outlets, a farmstall and a popular restaurant and pub.

This rather rustic corner of the peninsula is a fine example of Cape Town's natural heritage. To truly appreciate the splendour of the Atlantic seaboard, it is recommended that visitors take a leisurely drive back toward the city via Noordhoek and Hout Bay along Chapman's Peak Drive as the sun sets. The experience is quite unforgettable.

OPPOSITE TOP *From the comfort of a tour boat, visitors come face to face with Seal Island's famed inhabitants.*

OPPOSITE BOTTOM *The awe-inspiring scenic drive around Chapman's Peak is surpassed only by its superlative sunsets.*

ABOVE *The long, white beach at Noordhoek offers plenty of room for horseback riding, as well as other pursuits.*

USEFUL INFORMATION

Cape Town Stadium: Green Point, Visitors' Centre; tel: 021 400- 9140 (StadeFrance Operating Company)
Chapman's Peak Hotel: Chapman's Peak Dr., Hout Bay; tel: 021 790-1036; www.chapmanspeakhotel.co.za
Children's Recreational Park (Mini Train, Putt-Putt and Maze): 7 Beach Rd, Green Point; open 9am–5pm daily; tel: 021 434-8537
Circe Launches: tel: 021 790-1040; www.circelaunches.co.za
Hooked-on-Africa Fishing Tours: tel: 021 790-533; www.hookedonafrica.co.za
Hout Bay Information Centre: tel: 021 790-1264
Hout Bay Museum: 4 St Andrew's Rd; open 8am–4pm Mon–Fri; tel: 021 790-3270
Kitima Restaurant: tel: 021 790-8004
Noordhoek Farm Village: Main Rd, Noordhoek; tel: 021 789-1317
Noordhoek Tourism Office: Noordhoek Farm Village, Main Rd; tel: 021 789-2812; www.noordhoektourism.co.za
Noordhoek Village Farmstall: Noordhoek Farm Village, Main Rd; tel: 021 789-1390
South African Fisheries Museum: Hout Bay Harbour; open 8am–4pm Mon–Fri; tel: 021 790-7268
Suikerbossie: Off Victoria Ave, Hout Bay; tel: 021 790-1450; www.suikerbossie.co.za
Theatre on the Bay: 1 Links St, Camps Bay; tel: 021 438-3301; www.theatreonthebay.co.za
World of Birds: Valley Rd, Hout Bay; open 9am–5pm daily; tel 021 790-2730; www.worldofbirds.org.za

DAY
5

FALSE BAY

FALSE BAY

Muizenberg • St James • Kalk Bay • Fish Hoek • Simon's Town • Miller's Point • Smitswinkelbaai
Cape of Good Hope Nature Reserve • Scarborough • Kommetjie • Imhoff's Gift • Silvermine

The natural bay that stretches along the peninsula's eastern coastline from the Cape of Good Hope Nature Reserve at Cape Point to Cape Hangklip came to be known as False Bay because early navigators mistook Hangklip for Cape Point. The error resulted in many shipwrecks along this hazardous shoreline, but today the shores of False Bay are lined with small coastal towns, and the land varies from compact suburbia to long stretches of natural beach. Access to the area from the centre of Cape Town is via the Blue Route (M3), or along Prince George's Drive (M5), which extends as far as Muizenberg. The scenic mountain road via Boyes Drive, in turn, commands impressive views over the seaside suburbs of Muizenberg and St James. Visitors can follow the beautiful coastal route through Lakeside, Muizenberg, St James, Kalk Bay, Fish Hoek, and Simon's Town to Cape Point. Each route has its drawcards, but the most exciting must surely be the sight of the southern right whales that congregate between May and September in order to calve in the waters of False Bay.

Within the bay itself lies **Seal Island**, a breeding ground for both the Cape fur seal and many species of seabirds, and – because of the plentiful prey – the hunting ground of the great white shark. Although it is always advisable to be on the lookout for these much-feared – and often-seen – predators, few attacks have been reported in recent years, and even fewer have proven disastrous for bathers. Trained shark spotters operate from Boyes Drive, which winds across the mountainside above the bay, and will point out predators when they make their way into the bathing areas. For those who may want to take a closer look at these hunters of the seas, contact Cape-Xtreme, African Shark Eco Charters or White Shark Ecoventures.

Muizenberg
Nestled against the slopes of Muizenberg Mountain, 25 kilometres (15 miles) from the city, the town of **Muizenberg** has its origins in the very early days of the Cape when the coastal strip was first settled by Europeans. The Battle of Muizenberg

PREVIOUS PAGES *Jutting finger-like into the Atlantic Ocean is the appropriately named Cape Point, centrepiece of the scenic Cape of Good Hope Nature Reserve.*

INSET *The sometimes insolent antics of troops of resident chacma baboons delight visitors to Cape Point.*

ABOVE *The colony of jackass penguins that take refuge at Boulders Beach near Simon's Town are protected by law.*

OPPOSITE *Reminiscent of the 1920s, when the small seaside town was a popular resort, brightly painted bathing boxes line the small beach at St James.*

TOP *The warm waters of the False Bay feed into the Sandvlei Lagoon beneath the gaze of the surrounding mountains.*

MIDDLE *The coast at Muizenberg has long been a haunt of local fishermen who ply the waters of False Bay.*

ABOVE *Muizenberg's famed stretch of beach is a popular drawcard for surfers who flock to ride its impressive waves.*

was fought here in 1795 between the British and the Dutch. In the early years of the 20th century, Muizenberg became one of the country's most favoured holiday resorts, and a string of impressive homes was erected on the mountainside overlooking False Bay. Soon, however, many of the old Edwardian and Victorian homes were joined by representatives of more recent architectural styles. As a result, the modern township is a charming mix of old villas, fishermen's cottages and colonial structures – such as the fine red-brick Edwardian building on **Muizenberg Station**, with its grand spiral staircase (and now housing a restaurant) – and the modern elements, which include the 29-storey Cinnabar building and the **Muizenberg Promenade and Pavilion**.

The **Sandvlei Lagoon** area, which today seems to form the centre of the built-up area, was originally established as a cattle post. Today, the banks of the lagoon are lined with a small bird sanctuary to the north – and a variety of housing complexes. The most noticeable is the **Marina da Gama** development to the east. Sandvlei is fed by the salt water of the Atlantic, and the lagoon has become the domain of both waterfowl and watersport enthusiasts. Windsurfers, kiteboarders and canoeists ply the waters of the lagoon and the sea off Muizenberg.

Surfer's Corner Beach is one of the safest places in the country to learn to surf, attracting novices of all ages and genders. The beach is dotted with equipment-hire stores, coffee shops, change rooms, public toilets and plenty of parking. A waters-edge walkway – leading all the way over the rocks to St James in the west, and popular among afternoon strollers – and a promenade leading off to the east certainly make for a pleasant stroll. The modern concrete promenade replaced the original structure built in the early 1900s, and offers a splendid view over the ocean and the wave-lapped beaches – usually packed with bathers stretched out among the vibrant bathing huts erected on the beach in the late 19th century and recently renovated. From the promenade, spring visitors can also spot the whales gambolling in False Bay.

Although Muizenberg saw its heyday in the early 1900s when it served as a seaside retreat and popular holiday resort, and in the mid- to late-20th century began to fall into rapid decline, the future of the sadly neglected coastal town is looking bright. Despite a number of well-intentioned proposals to rejuvenate Muizenberg over the years, many of its seedier corners are at last seeing some sign of revival. Following a steady trickle of interest in the seaside homes in recent years, and even the shooting of international movies along its seafront, the suburb is now considered one of the up-and-coming investment areas on the peninsula. Already, the 1920 structures and impressive Art Deco homes and shopfronts that line the beach have been or are in the process of being renovated, and quite a few of the residential hotels have been converted into chic accommodation units.

The small whitewashed cottage known as **Het Post Huijs** on Main Road was built in 1673, and is the oldest inhabitable

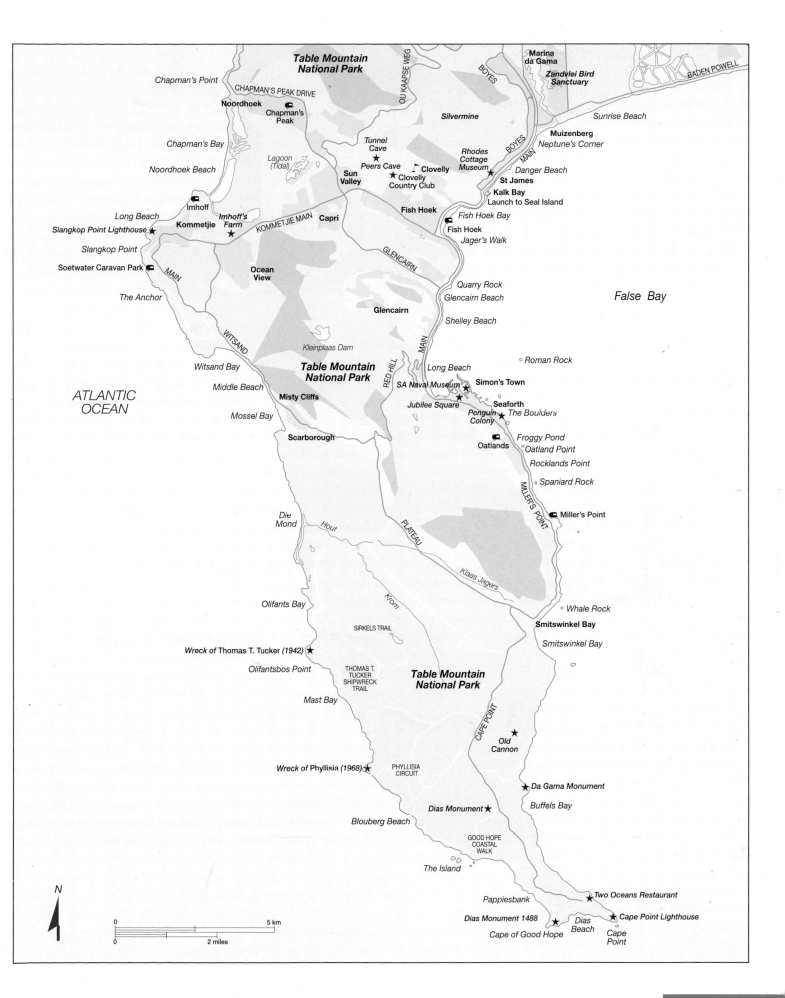

Table Mountain
National Park

Chapman's Point

CHAPMAN'S PEAK DRIVE

Noordhoek

Chapman's
Peak

Chapman's Bay

Noordhoek Beach

OU KAAPSE WEG

BOYES

Marina
da Gama

Zandvlei Bird
Sanctuary

BADEN POWELL

Silvermine

BOYES

MAIN

Muizenberg

Neptune's Corner

Sunrise Beach

Tunnel
Cave

Peers Cave

Rhodes
Cottage
Museum

Danger Beach

Clovelly

Sun
Valley

Clovelly
Country Club

St James

Kalk Bay

Launch to Seal Island

Lagoon
(Tidal)

Imhoff

Long Beach

Slangkop Point Lighthouse

Kommetjie

Imhoff's
Farm

KOMMETJIE MAIN

Capri

Fish Hoek

Fish Hoek Bay

Fish Hoek

Jager's Walk

Slangkop Point

MAIN

Ocean
View

GLENCAIRN

Quarry Rock

Glencairn Beach

False Bay

Soetwater Caravan Park

The Anchor

Glencairn

Shelley Beach

WITSAND

Kleinplaas Dam

Table Mountain
National Park

RED HILL

MAIN

Roman Rock

Long Beach

SA Naval Museum

Simon's Town

Witsand Bay

Middle Beach

Misty Cliffs

Jubilee Square

Seaforth

The Boulders

ATLANTIC
OCEAN

Penguin
Colony

Mossel Bay

Froggy Pond

Scarborough

Oatlands

Oatland Point

Rocklands Point

Spaniard Rock

MILLER'S POINT

Miller's Point

Die
Mond

Hout

PLATEAU

Klaas Jagers

Olifants Bay

Krom

Whale Rock

SIRKELS TRAIL

Smitswinkel Bay

Smitswinkel Bay

Wreck of Thomas T. Tucker (1942)

Olifantsbos Point

THOMAS T.
TUCKER
SHIPWRECK
TRAIL

Table Mountain
National Park

Mast Bay

CAPE POINT

Old
Cannon

Wreck of Phyllisia (1968)

PHYLLISIA
CIRCUIT

Da Gama Monument

Dias Monument

Buffels Bay

Blouberg Beach

GOOD HOPE
COASTAL
WALK

The Island

N

Two Oceans Restaurant

Pappiesbank

Dias Monument 1488

Dias
Beach

Cape Point Lighthouse

Cape of Good Hope

Cape
Point

0   5 km

0   2 miles

European house in the country, predating even the Castle of Good Hope. It was originally used as a signal station, house and fort under the auspices of the Dutch East India Company (VOC), and today it houses an exhibition devoted to the story of the Battle of Muizenberg.

The Italian-style building at number 192 Main Road was once the home of Count Natale Labia. Further along the recently upgraded Main Road is the equally impressive **Rust-en-Vrede**, the home of mining tycoon Sir Abe Bailey and designed by Sir Herbert Baker. It remains a private home so is not open for viewing, but certainly worth a visit is the little stone bungalow at number 246, which stands out among the many imposing houses stretching down the mountainside. This is the **Rhodes Cottage Museum**, the holiday home of Cape premier and tycoon Cecil John Rhodes. The simple house displays items of Rhodes's personal memorabilia.

The steep mountain slopes and extreme shortage of land along this scenic coastal strip skirting False Bay mean that, yet again, property prices have rocketed in recent years. At the same time, however, some of the older residential hotels and holiday accommodation – many requiring more than a simple lick of paint to restore them to the grandeur they enjoyed at the turn of the last century – have given way to contemporary developments such as up-market apartment blocks and smaller, more exclusive boutique hotels and bed-and-breakfasts. While this has indeed changed the old-world character, it is seen by many as a welcome improvement.

St James

Legend has it that the first parish priest stationed at the St James Catholic Church, erected in 1854, refused to accept his post unless a railway station was established to encourage parishioners to attend mass. Needless to say, the railway station and the suburb that grew up around it all became known as **St James**, and the church still serves Catholic worshippers from near and far.

Largely because of limited building space on the mountain slopes and narrow verges, St James has seen relatively little development. Situated as it is at the foot of Kalk Bay Mountain (Kalkbaaiberg), St James and its surroundings remain immensely attractive. The natural beauty encompasses not only Kalkbaaiberg – the mountain's original Dutch name – but also a number of natural features such as rock pools, small waterfalls, streams and caves – for instance, Tartarus, Erica and Jubilee – making it ideal for casual walks, hikes and bird-watching. Visitors should, however, consult with professional guides before attempting to enter any of the caves as they are

notorioulsy treacherous and home to many rare, protected plant and animal species. The plotted walk through the Spes-Bona Valley Forest starts at Boyes Drive above St James and takes hikers past splendid wild olive trees, indigenous yellowwoods and the rooi els (red elder) for which the area has become so well known, and ends at Tartarus Cave.

The small, sheltered stretch of sand on the seaward side of Main Road below is dotted with brightly coloured bathing boxes, much like those at Muizenberg, and is popular with children. It has a multitude of tiny rock pools and, of course, a walled tidal pool. Surfers congregate at Danger Beach, which is a little further south.

Kalk Bay

A surfing mecca with a decidedly bohemian atmosphere, the fishing village of Kalk Bay was first inhabited by Europeans in the 1600s when shipwrecked sailors took refuge in the many caves that dot the mountainside. The bay is named for the kilns built by the VOC in which seashells were burned to make lime for building cement – 'kalk' is the Dutch word for lime. In the early 19th century, the protected bay below Trappiekop on Kalkbaaiberg became an active harbour catering largely for the fishermen and whalers who worked the southern coast. The

slopes of the mountain are still dotted with the humble homes of the descendants of these fisherfolk. A small fleet of brightly painted fishing vessels continues to ply the southern waters for snoek and other fish.

The fishermen return to Kalk Bay with their catch around noon. The fish is always straight out of the water, and definitely worth the price. If you aren't prepared to gut and descale the fish yourself, the fishermen will do it for you. Visitors can even take a trip out with the fishermen (contact the harbour master), but an easier way to sample the local dishes is to visit the nearby **Brass Bell** restaurant. Because this restaurant and pub are situated on Kalk Bay railway station, visitors may want to take the train from Cape Town central station. Just a few metres away from the harbour, the Brass Bell has become well known for its superb menu, and especially for its seafood. More recent – and highly notable – additions to the Kalk Bay restaurant scene include the **Polana** and **Harbour House**, both situated magnificently on the harbour wall, and the world-renowned yet delightfully local **Olympia Café & Deli**.

The main coastal road that runs through Kalk Bay is lined with quaint shops and cafés, each specialising in something different: ceramics, paintings, driftwood art, bric-a-brac, antiques (both genuine and not quite authentic) and other remnants of a bygone era.

Fish Hoek

The little hamlet of **Fish Hoek** was established in 1918, but has grown considerably in recent years. Fish Hoek is most noted for its long, gentle beach and for whale viewing in late winter and early spring. The beach (now a pay

LEFT *Fishing boats moored on the still waters of Kalk Bay Harbour.*

ABOVE *The train line sweeps along the rocky coast at the foot of Kalk Bay Mountain as it winds toward Fish Hoek.*

False Bay

beach) is popular with dog-walkers, while kite-fliers converge on the sands on the frequent windy days. On sunny days bathers flock to this picturesque strip – set aside as a marine reserve, like the rest of the False Bay coast – and the warm waters are suited to both surfing and sailing. Anglers congregate on the rocks nearby or try their luck from small boats further out in the bay. Among the facilities are changing rooms, ablution facilities and even a playground and restaurant. Life in this town is decidedly laid-back and relaxing; a popular pastime is a stroll along **Jager's Walk**, a concrete catwalk that stretches along the rocky shoreline from Fish Hoek towards Simon's Town, offering panoramic views of the Bay.

The business area of central Fish Hoek is rather like a small village, the Main Road running right through a small enclave of shops that range from large national chainstores to small gift shops, craft outlets and suppliers of sporting goods and the like.

The mountain slopes behind Fish Hoek reach as far as Noordhoek Valley. In **Peers Cave** – follow the signs from 20th Avenue – a number of ancient burial sites were discovered by Victor Peers in 1927. Surrounded by San rock paintings on the cave walls, the oldest specimen is at least 12 000 years old and the ancient remains have since become known as Fish Hoek Man. The primitive stone implements and artefacts found here may still be viewed at the **Fish Hoek Valley Museum** on Central Circle. The museum also arranges organised hiking trails within the area.

Beyond Fish Hoek lies the picturesque, seaside village of **Simon's Town**, home base of the South African Navy. It is possible to bypass the town via Red Hill directly to Scarborough. However, it is worthwhile driving through Simon's Town. Just beyond the turnoff to the grave of Able Seaman Just Nuisance outside the South African Naval Signal School is the road up Simonsberg, which provides an excellent vantage point from which to view the bay below. The road leads right into the little village of Scarborough on the Atlantic seaboard. Visitors should be aware that, for security reasons, they are not allowed to photograph the naval base.

En Route to Simon's Town

Just before you reach Simon's Town – on Dido Valley Road off Red Hill Road – lies the world's biggest polished gemstone factory. At **Topstones**, polishing and tumbling machines turn rough rocks into semi-precious stones. The plant is open to the public and is very popular with children who scramble through the mounds of polished and unpolished stones searching for the perfect gem. Purchase a bucket upon entry, and you are allowed to take home all that the container can hold.

From here the road to Simon's Town has a clear view over the bay and is a favourite spot for whale watching during the calving season. Also dotted along this rugged coastline are traces of the many ships that have come to grief on the rocky shores over the centuries, among them the SS *Clan Stuart, Bato, Die Gebroeders, Katwyk Aan Rhyn, Parama* and the *Phoenix* on the other side of Selbourne Dry Dock. The expanse of white sand – aptly named Long Beach – that stretches along this route has long been the playground of the inhabitants of Simon's Town as well as visitors to the area. Long Beach ends at the station – the last stop on the Southern Suburbs railway line – at the entrance to the town.

Early Simon's Town

The historic town traces its origins to Simon van der Stel who, as governor of the relatively new settlement, decided that the bay was an ideal harbour for the Dutch fleet during the winter months. It was, however, only after Baron von Imhoff set up a

TOP *Fishermen like this one set out each day from the fishing village of Kalk Bay. The arrival of the catch is a daily highlight.*

LEFT *The Boulders, near Simon's Town, offers the endearing sight of a mother African penguin fussing over one of her chicks.*

OPPOSITE TOP *The long, gentle, sun-drenched beach at Fish Hoek draws plenty of watersport enthusiasts and bathers.*

OPPOSITE BOTTOM *A port since the earliest days of European settlement, Simon's Town is the base of the South African Navy.*

proper port and dockland here in 1743 that Simon's Bay began to take on the naval responsibilities it enjoys today. For nearly 150 years, the town was the South Atlantic base for the Royal Navy, and only came under South African control in 1957. The naval influence is still very much in evidence. Uniformed naval personnel stroll the same cobbled pavements as sailors of old, and many of the townsfolk are employed by the navy or the adjoining dockyard.

Simon's Town, however, is not only a bastion of the military, but provides a delightful look into the history of the country. Although the main road running through the village changes its name at regular intervals – Main Road becomes Station Road, St George's Street, Queens Road, Macfarlane Road and back to Main – it is indeed a single road, and one crammed with memories of yesteryear. The Simon's Town information office can offer advice as well as brochures on accommodation, sightseeing and any number of guided walks and tours covering the historic route and hikes through the fynbos of Simonsberg.

Many of the oldest parts of the town and especially the working dockyard date back to the early days of the Cape. The Lower North Battery was built by the Dutch over 200 years ago, and today serves as the Gunnery School's firing range, while the West Dockyard was the site of the first store and naval hospital selected by Baron von Imhoff.

Simon's Town Today

The first place of interest on entering the town, and certainly one of its most famous, is elegant **Admiralty House** off Station Road, historically the home of the naval commander and now open to the public. The gabled manor was built in typical Cape Regency style by VOC official Antoni Vissir in the early 19th century and served as the Cape residence of visiting naval officials, ships' captains, royalty and other distinguished travellers until it was sold to the Royal Navy.

False Bay

Perhaps one of the most charming old buildings in Simon's Town is the **Church of St Francis** on Court Road, which dates back to 1837. According to local legend, the little church may be the oldest Anglican church in the country, and was consecrated five years after its construction by the visiting Bishop of Tasmania. Originally named after Lady Frances Cole, who helped raise the money required to build the church, the name has since been changed to commemorate Francis of Assisi, the patron saint of animals.

Court Road is also home to **The Residency**, which now houses the **Simon's Town Museum** and the tourism and information office. Over the years, the building has served as the offices of the magistrate, the governor's retreat, a hospital, slave quarters and a prison – see the cells and the stocks in which prisoners were confined – but today it tells the story of the town and particularly its naval connection.

Jubilee Square is the heart of Simon's Town, and its busy arcade of shops, market stalls and cafés looks down over the harbour. It is on this public square that the bronze statue of Able Seaman Just Nuisance commemorates one of the town's most famous residents. Many ships have mascots but none achieved such fame as that of HMS *Neptune* and HMS *Afrikander I*, the Great Dane who 'enlisted' in the Royal Navy in 1939. The dog was so loved by his comrades-in-arms during the war that, on his death in 1943, Just Nuisance, wrapped in the White Ensign, was buried with full naval honours.

To the north of Jubilee Square is the **False Bay Yacht Club** – offering yachts and fishing boats for charter – and, to the right, the old **Stempastorie**. This was originally the home of the resident Dutch Reformed minister and where, in 1919, the Reverend Marthinus de Villiers wrote the score for *Die Stem* (The Voice), once the national anthem of South Africa and now joint anthem with *Nkosi Sikeleli Africa* (God Bless Africa). The old Stempastorie was once a museum, but it is no longer open to the public.

The **Warrior Toy Museum** on St George's Street will undoubtedly be popular with the little ones, as it boasts a wide collection of both antique and more recent children's toys, including old dolls, trains and original lead soldiers dating back to the 1700s.

Roman Rock Lighthouse in Simon's Bay was erected in 1861 to guide the increasing number of ships visiting Simon's Town into the precarious bay. Still in working order, it is said to be the third oldest lighthouse in South Africa, and the only one to be purposely built on a rock.

The Simon's Town Harbour is worth a visit, particularly the West Dockyard and in it, the **Martello Tower** and **Naval Museum**. The exhibits here cover naval ships, South Africa's maritime history and the story of the men and women who served in the country's fleet. There is also an authentic recreation of a pub as it would have looked during the World War II, and displays of mementoes left by Lord Nelson, hero of the Battle of Trafalgar in 1805.

Nearing the southern limit of Simon's Town is popular **Seaforth Beach**, one of the last on this route to cater for the needs of families. Bathing in the crystal waters of this protected beach is quite safe, and there are lawns for picnicking, a parking area and a waterslide.

The coastline beyond Simon's Town holds little historic value but its natural beauty is considered by many to be unsurpassed on the peninsula. The flora and fauna here have been virtually untouched by humankind, and much of it is protected by law. Just outside Simon's Town is the secluded enclave of **Boulders Beach**, known also as The Boulders, or simply Boulders. The beach is home to a colony of endangered African penguins, and is protected by the massive rounded granite outcrops from which it gets its name. The waters of this sheltered beach are both warm and safe. There is a small entrance fee to the penguin rookery. One of the few human intrusions permitted along this coast is the Simon's Town Country Club and golf course, situated between Simon's Town and Miller's Point.

Miller's Point and Smitswinkelbaai

Beyond Froggy Farm and Murdock Valley, with its well-known and appropriately named Fishermen's Beach, lies beautiful Miller's Point. The area buzzes with activity in spring, when southern right, humpback and Bryde's whales congregate at the point. There is a caravan park – generally booked up in the holiday season – and a tidal pool, and it is here, too, that crayfish divers and snorkellers converge to either harvest the plentiful crustaceans or explore the marine life. Miller's Point is home to the **Black Marlin Seafood Restaurant** – one of the city's most highly acclaimed seafood restaurants.

Just off the point where the road turns back into the Cape of Good Hope Nature Reserve lies tranquil **Smitswinkelbaai**, a cosy enclave of private cottages inaccessible by road. The waters of this bay are ideal for both swimming and fishing, but there is a steep path leading to the beach.

The short route between Smitswinkelbaai and the gates to the Cape of Good Hope Nature Reserve has its own attractions. The winding road ascends, providing spectacular views of the precipitous coastline and the waters of False Bay. Just outside the entrance to the reserve, visitors will find an open-air roadside market crammed with carved animals, African masks and wooden statuettes – most produced in Zimbabwe. Just 500

metres (1 640 feet) beyond the reserve gates is the Cape Point Ostrich Farm. Although primarily a working farm – there is no ostrich riding or racing offered – visitors are welcome to wander through this former chicken farm, which has been renovated to cater for the breeding of these strange-looking flightless birds. Tours include the incubators, hatchery and rearing pens. Naturally, choice cuts of ostrich meat figure on the menu at the farm restaurant, and leather and feather products are available at the shop.

Cape of Good Hope Nature Reserve

Encompassing the entire southern tip of the peninsula and Cape Point, the **Cape of Good Hope Nature Reserve** – in the Table Mountain National Park – is a protected paradise only an hour's drive from the city centre and is visited by more than 400 000 people every year. The 40 kilometres (25 miles) of the reserve's coastline extends from Smitswinkelbaai on False Bay through Buffelsbaai, Cape Point, Mast Bay, Olifantsbospunt and Schuster Bay to Scarborough on the Atlantic seaboard. Entrance to the reserve is limited to a single road and the conservation of the ecosystem is a high priority for the custodians. Although picnic and braai facilities have been specially designated for public use and there are a number of signposted walking routes and places of interest, all the normal rules pertaining to protected areas apply. Visitors to the marine reserve are permitted to leave their car – except, of course, in the restricted areas – but are warned that officials do not take kindly to the damage that is done either to the natural environment or the animals that are found there, nor to unlawful fishing and crayfishing within its waters.

The baboons often encountered along the roadside have become so accustomed to handouts from curious onlookers

---

OPPOSITE *Many of the charming arcaded buildings lining Simon's Town's Main Road date back to the 19th century.*

TOP *In a city renowned for its seafood, one of the finest seafood menus is offered by the Black Marlin, near Miller's Point.*

RIGHT *The only canine to enlist in the Royal Navy, Able Seaman Just Nuisance is commemorated with a statue on Jubilee Square.*

that their natural instinct to hunt has been replaced by the need to scavenge. As a result, they can be very aggressive in their determination to feed, and have been known to attack. Visitors are warned not to open car windows or to offer the baboons food. All visitors are advised to pick up a copy of the visitors' rules available at the information kiosk at the reserve entrance.

The reserve's nearly 8 000-hectare (19 768-acre) area is home to over a thousand different floral species and a wealth of wildlife. Among the smaller species to be found here are the dassie, Cape fox and baboon. Larger mammals include Cape mountain zebra and a variety of antelope species, such as the endangered bontebok – which is endemic to the southwestern Cape – and eland. The waters are inhabited by migrating whales, dolphins and seals.

The halfway mark between Smitswinkelbaai and Cape Point is picturesque **Buffelsbaai**, the starting point for some splendid walks among the fynbos and rocky landscape. Buffelsbaai has its own slipway for fishing boats, as well as picnicking facilities and a tidal pool. There is a shipwreck just off the coast, and angling is permitted from the beach.

On the rocky shore stands a monument to Vasco da Gama. Just inland is the stone cross erected in memory of Bartolomeu Dias, the first European explorer to view – but not land on – this remote area of the Cape. Dias first named the peninsula the Cape of Storms, but then changed it to the Cape of Good Hope as he neared the end of his journey, which he hoped would lead him to the rich trading grounds of the East. It is said that when the two memorials are lined up, they indicate the location of the much-feared Whittle Rock. At Olifantsbospunt, about halfway between Cape Point and Scarborough, are the wrecks of the *Thomas T. Tucker*, which ran aground here in 1942, and the *Nolloth*, which sank in 1965 at nearby Duikerklip.

Cape Point

The southern tip of the Cape Peninsula is not, despite popular belief, the meeting place of the Indian and Atlantic oceans; this

---

TOP RIGHT *The scenic wonder of Cape Point draws large numbers of tourists to its awe-inspiring views of the Atlantic Ocean.*

MIDDLE RIGHT *The Cape of Good Hope Nature Reserve provides a protected haven for animals such as the Cape bontebok.*

BOTTOM RIGHT *Cape Point's Two Oceans Restaurant offers diners panoramic views of False Bay's majestic coastline.*

OPPOSITE TOP *The old lighthouse at Cape Point is today a prime vantage point.*

OPPOSITE BOTTOM *A funicular railway offers visitors a less taxing route up to the lookout at Cape Point.*

honour is reserved for Cape Agulhas, the southernmost point of Africa. Visitors will often encounter this myth, yet if ever there was a place which could be forgiven for perpetuating the myth, it is Cape Point. The natural beauty and superlative views provide one of the wonders of the peninsula, and visitors flock here to take photographs, breathe the sea air, admire the fynbos and walk the unspoilt terrain.

Dias Beach, shielded by cliffs, may be reached only via a rugged flight of steps, but the panorama that awaits is exceptional. From Dias, the highest sea cliffs in the country tower up to the point and lighthouse. But some of the best views must surely be those from the shop and restaurant complex on the cliffs near the main parking area. From here, the views across to Muizenberg may take your breath away. The curio shop and the popular **Two Oceans Restaurant** are located here. There is also a snack bar and information desk at the lower station of the funicular railway, which ferries visitors up to the old lighthouse at the top of the point. At the top of the funicular, there is another shop and an information centre housed in the former home of the lighthouse keeper.

The 300-metre (985-foot) cliffs fall straight down from the lookout platform above, and the view from here extends across False Bay to Danger Point, some 80 kilometres (50 miles) to the east. This is also the site of the old 2 000-candlepower lighthouse that was erected in 1861 and served for 50 years. After the Portuguese liner *Lusitania* foundered on Bellows Rock below in 1911, a second lighthouse was built further down in 1914. This new lighthouse, which was electrified in 1936, may be seen from viewpoints at the upper station.

Scarborough and Kommetjie

The sleepy seaside village of **Scarborough** is an idyllic getaway. Just beyond Scarborough is majestic **Misty Cliffs**. There are plenty of picnic areas around here, but don't miss the food at **Camel Rock** restaurant on Main Road. The vegetarian fare and seafood dishes are a treat.

Nearby Witsand – between Scarborough and the Slangkop Point Lighthouse – is quite tiny, but makes for a charming diversion. Although the rustic Soetwater Caravan Park has no electrical power, it does boast other amenities such as overnight camping facilities, caravan stands, a tidal pool and picnic spots.

Kommetjie is a little closer to what most travellers would call 'civilisation'. The little fishing village, dotted with milkwood trees, was established at the turn of the century and is a mecca for watersport enthusiasts, with surfers, waveskiers, windsurfers and anglers flocking to the area. Like Scarborough and the rest of the southern peninsula, the natural heritage here is relatively untouched, with only a scattering of holiday homes. Apart from the magnificent stretch of white sand that is Long Beach – which incorporates both Klein Slangpunt and Bokramstrand – other attractions include the **Slangkop Point Lighthouse,** which dates from 1919, and the wreck of the *Kakapo*, a steamship that ran aground on its maiden voyage in 1900 when its captain made the fatal error of mistaking Chapman's Peak for Cape Point.

Imhoff's Gift, between Kommetjie/Ocean View and Noordhoek is a pleasant reminder of days gone by. Originally the property of Baron von Imhoff, Commissioner of the VOC in 1743, who established the port at Simon's Town, the buildings have been turned into a unique community centre. There are several offbeat shops, a farmstall, a tea garden and camel or horse rides for the children. The **nature park and wildlife sanctuary**, which forms part of **Imhoff Farm**, houses giants of the bird world such as ostriches, emus and blue cranes. Right next door is the **Snake & Reptile Park**, offering a rare close look at snakes from all over the world, in addition to spiders and a host of other reptiles.

The fynbos vegetation that stretches along the roadside and up the mountain slopes here is indigenous to the region and forms part of the Cape Floral Kingdom that covers much of the Table Mountain National Park, which was declared a World Heritage Site in 2004. The national park extends across the peninsula from Lion's Head to Cape Point and there are a number of new walking trails for visitors to

enjoy. Visitors should be aware that the vegetation it harbours must not be disturbed as it is protected by law.

part of which is occupied by a South African Navy base. In 2000, a devastating fire raged through the area destroying vast tracts of fynbos. This prompted the authorities to undertake a massive clean-up of alien vegetation – the main propellant of veld fires – in

Silvermine

The scenic route from Kommetjie and surrounds takes the traveller along Kommetjie Road towards Fish Hoek and then left onto one of the most magnificent stretches of road in the Cape. Both the setting and the views along **Ou Kaapse Weg** – meaning 'Old Cape Road' – are quite extraordinary as it winds along the mountainside and through the **Silvermine** section of Table Mountain National Park. Its steep gradient is also the most punishing segment of the famed Cape Argus Pick n Pay Cycle Tour. The reserve covers much of what was the original silver mine initiated by Governor Simon van der Stel in 1687, when he sent prospectors on a fruitless search for the precious metal.

There are a number of points of entry from Ou Kaapse Weg into the section,

the area and throughout the peninsula. Today, the conservation area encompasses some of the finest expanses of fynbos vegetation and other Cape flora in the peninsula. Silvermine's wildlife includes a diversity of birds – among them the black eagle – and mammal species varying from antelopes such as grysbok and rhebok to genets, porcupines and baboons, plus an array of insects, amphibians and reptiles including the reclusive puff adder.

The area to the west of the Ou Kaapse Weg leads to the source of the Silvermine River – **Noordhoek Peak,** at about 750 metres (2 460 feet) above sea level, and the highest point in Silvermine. The panorama from here stretches along Chapman's Peak Drive to The Sentinel in Hout Bay. On the eastern side of Ou Kaapse Weg lie the mountains of Muizenberg and Kalkbaaiberg and a view that embraces False Bay, the Southern Suburbs and Constantia, Table Mountain and across the Cape Flats to the Strand.

ABOVE *From the Cape Point lighthouse, visitors are afforded a spectacular view of the Cape of Good Hope.*

OPPOSITE BOTTOM *The tidal pools of Scarborough are home to large beds of the black mussels so popular on local menus.*

USEFUL INFORMATION

African Shark Eco Charters: tel: 021 785-1947; www.ultimate-animals.com

Camel Rock Restaurant: Main Rd, Scarborough; tel: 021 780-1122

Cape-Xtreme: tel: 021 422-4198; www.cape-xtreme.com

Cape of Good Hope Nature Reserve: Open 6am–6pm daily (Oct–Mar), 7am–5pm daily (Apr–Sept); tel: 021 780-9204; www.tmnp.co.za

Cape Point Information Centre: tel: 021 780-9204; www.tmnp.co.za

Cape Point Ostrich Farm: Bonne Attente Farm, Cape Point; open 9.30am–5.30pm daily; cpof@iafrica.com; tel: 021 780-9294; www.capepointostrichfarm.com

Cape Town Tourism (Muizenberg Office): Pavilion Building, Beach Rd; peninsula@tourismcapetown.co.za; tel: 021 788-6176; www.tourismcapetown.co.za

Cape Town Tourism (Simon's Town Office): 111 St George's St, Simon's Town; open 9am–5pm Mon–Fri, 9.30am–1pm Sat; simonstown@tourismcapetown.co.za; tel: 021 786-2436/5798; www.capetown.co.za

Church of St Francis of Assisi: Contact Pastor Basil Adams tel: 021 786-3564

False Bay Yacht Club: King George Way, Simon's Town; tel: 021 786-1703; www.fbyc.co.za

Fish Hoek Valley Museum: 59 Central Circle; open 9.30am–12.30pm Tues–Sat; tel: 021 782-1752

Het Post Huijs: Main Rd, Muizenberg; open 10am–2pm daily; tel: 021 788-7772

Imhoff Farm: Kommetjie Rd, Kommetjie; open 9am–5pm Tues–Sun; tel: 021 783-4545; www.imhofffarm.co.za

Kalk Bay Harbour (Harbour Master): Main Rd; kalkbay@deat.gov.za; tel: 021 788-8313; www.mcm-deat.gov.za

Polana Restaurant: Kalk Bay Harbour; tel: 021 788-7162

Rhodes Cottage Museum: 246 Main Rd, Muizenberg; open 10am–3.30pm daily (May–Aug), 9.30am–4.30pm daily (Sept–Apr); tel: 021 788-1816

Silvermine: Ou Kaapseweg, Tokai; open 8am–6pm daily; tel: 021 780-9002

Simon's Town Museum: 56 Court Rd; open 9am–4pm Mon–Fri, 10am–1pm Sat, 11am–3pm Sun; museummc@mweb.co.za; tel: 021 786-3046; www.simonstown.com

Soetwater Caravan Park: tel: 021 783-1746

South African Naval Museum: St George's St, West Dockyard, Simon's Town; open 10am–4pm daily; tel: 021 787-4686

Topstones Mineral World: Dido Valley Rd, Simon's Town; open 8.30am–4.45pm Mon–Fri, 9am–5.30pm Sat–Sun; topstones@topstones.co.za; tel: 021 786-2020

Two Oceans Restaurant: Cape of Good Hope, Cape Point; tel: 021 780-9200

Warrior Toy Museum: St George's St, Simon's Town; open 10am–4pm daily; tel: 021 786-1395

False Bay

DAY
6

CONSTANTIA &
THE SOUTHERN SUBURBS

CONSTANTIA & THE SOUTHERN SUBURBS

Rhodes Memorial • Rosebank • Rondebosch • Newlands • Claremont • Wynberg • Constantia
Groot Constantia • Constantia Nek • Rondevlei Nature Reserve

The Southern Suburbs lie in the shadow of the mountain ranges that form the spine of the peninsula. Situated in what is known as the Green Belt – the average rainfall at the foot of the mountains tends to be higher than in the rest of the Cape – the lush suburbs provide not only a peek at Capetonians at home, but also a revealing look into the history of the city itself, particularly during the days of English and Dutch occupation. As a result, this string of residential areas reflects a broad and eclectic combination of influences, mixing magnificent Cape Dutch architecture with the Georgian and Victorian styles brought from England.

Access routes to the suburbs at the foot of Table Mountain are plentiful and varied. From the city, take either Eastern Boulevard or De Waal Drive – the latter changes its name regularly along the route, but follow the signs for the Southern Suburbs. As its name implies, Main Road is an important (if sometimes crowded and slow) route, which snakes through most of the Southern Suburbs. From the False Bay area, take the Blue Route (the M3 highway).

On his death in 1906, Cecil John Rhodes, premier of the Cape Colony, left the **Rhodes Estate** on the eastern slopes of Table Mountain to the nation. The land originally extended to the site of today's Groote Schuur Hospital, and includes such famed landmarks as **Mostert's Mill**, Rhodes Memorial and the **Groote Schuur Estate**.

The Slopes of Table Mountain

Travelling from the city to the suburbs on De Waal Drive past Devil's Peak, an expanse of open land stretches up the slopes. This sanctuary is part of Table Mountain National Park, and on sunny days small herds of grazing mountain zebra dot the landscape, unperturbed by the city traffic on the highway below.

Perhaps the most famous structure on this portion of the mountain is the grand monument built in commemoration of Cecil John Rhodes. Rhodes was only 18 when he and his brother staked their first claims on the diamond fields of Kimberley, but by the time he died he had created the world's most successful mining house, amassed an immense fortune,

PREVIOUS PAGES *The rural solitude of Buitenverwachting makes it the ideal setting for one of the Cape's most respected restaurants.*

INSET *Many of the famed old homesteads of Constantia are dated by the distinctive gables of the manor houses.*

ABOVE *The verandah-enclosed shrine of Sayed Mahmud is situated on the summit of Constantia's tranquil Islam Hill.*

OPPOSITE *Shrouded in lush greenery, Klein Constantia is one of the peninsula's premier wine estates.*

and even given his name to a country (Rhodesia, now Zimbabwe), acquiring along the way a reputation as a ruthless businessman, imperialist and politician.

The temple-like **Rhodes Memorial** was executed by Sir Herbert Baker in grand neo-Classical style, and was constructed in 1912 from Table Mountain granite. The centrepiece of the upper, colonnaded section is JW Swan's bust of Rhodes, inscribed with the words penned by Rudyard Kipling in honour of the statesman. At the foot of the monument's stone steps, which are guarded by eight massive bronze lions, stands an impressive equestrian statue, sculpted by GF Watts, titled *Physical Energy*. The view from the steps is quite breathtaking, taking in the city and immediate suburbs below, the Cape Flats, Tygerberg Hills and the distant Hottentots-Holland Mountains.

Tucked away behind the memorial and surrounded by the mountain's unique flora, stands a charming old stone cottage that serves as a restaurant and tearoom. The tiny lodge is particularly popular for afternoon tea and as a venue for intimate receptions. Just a little further up the slopes of the mountain, a small Prayer Garden is open to the public.

Below Rhodes Memorial, visitors will notice the characteristic sails of a traditional Dutch windmill at the turn-off from Rhodes Drive into Woolsack Drive, which leads down the hill into the suburb of Rosebank. This is **Mostert's Mill**, a rare example of an authentic Dutch windmill. The mill was built in 1796 by Wouter Mostert, one of the small number of free burghers who were permitted by Commander Jan van Riebeeck to establish farms beyond the immediate confines of the settlement on Table Bay. The mill was later purchased by the Van Reenen family of the farm Welgelegen. With financial aid from the Netherlands, the structure was painstakingly restored in 1936 and today Mostert's Mill is open to the public.

Observatory to Rosebank

The **South African Astronomical Observatory**, located off Observatory Road, has given its name to the bohemian suburb of Observatory. Built in 1820, the facility hosts plenty of activities related to the observation of the skies, and offers guided tours of the observatory itself. At 8pm every second Saturday, the observatory invites visitors to watch the stars over the city through its telescope.

The **Irma Stern Museum** on Cecil Road in Rosebank is a satellite of the University of Cape Town's fine art department, and provides considerable insight into the work and life of one of South Africa's most gifted painters. More than 200 of her paintings are exhibited in the house, which was her home for nearly 40 years. Born in Germany, Irma Stern was at times a controversial figure, but her passionate brushstrokes and exciting use of colour have ensured that her work remains highly regarded and much sought after. The museum also houses her collections of African, European and Eastern art and furniture, which she accumulated during her extensive travels. Her studio – which has been left undisturbed since her death in 1966 – is also the venue for temporary exhibitions of contemporary art.

Opposite The columned grandeur of Rhodes Memorial is an impressive reminder of one of the country's key historical figures.

Above The view over Cape Town and its suburbs from Rhodes Memorial is undeniably inspiring.

Right Sculpted by GF Watts, the statue of Physical Energy *stands boldly in the centre of the memorial to Rhodes.*

Rondebosch

Almost around the corner from the Irma Stern Museum, off Woolsack Drive on the Main Road, stands the University of Cape Town's **Baxter Theatre Centre**. Opened in 1977, the Baxter's theatres are the venue for the most prominent local stage productions. The main theatre concentrates on the more lavish and spectacular shows and musicals. Performances in the concert hall vary from dramatic productions to popular and classical music recitals, while the Golden Arrow Studio hosts experimental drama and cabarets. Local art is sometimes exhibited in the foyer, and there is both a restaurant and bar catering for the after-theatre crowd.

The most prominent landmark in the Rondebosch/Rosebank area – and, indeed, in the whole of the Southern Suburbs – is the **University of Cape Town**, the academic home of some 22 000 students. This array of sandstone buildings stands on the slopes of Devil's Peak, and houses the upper campus of South Africa's oldest university.

The other great landmark in Rondebosch is the **Groote Schuur Estate**. Meaning 'great barn', the Cape Dutch manor house was originally

built by Jan van Riebeeck to store the colony's all-important grain supply. When Cecil John Rhodes bought the granary, he had Sir Herbert Baker execute the renovations that we see today. The mansion – which is not open to the public – still houses the artworks and texts left behind by Rhodes for the nation.

As you travel further south, Main Road seems to split, creating a small 'island' in the middle of the road. On the left is the Riverside shopping centre and the old Rondebosch Fountain, a charming reminder of the ornate Victorian era. On the right, in the centre of the island, stands the stone chapel of **St Paul's Anglican Church**.

Newlands

Home to the country's most famous playing fields, the green suburb of Newlands, like much of the Southern Suburbs, is lined with avenues of oaks and is sheltered by the great bulk of the mountain. Through the tranquil suburb winds the Liesbeek River, along the banks of which stands the **Josephine Mill** on Boundary Road. Built in 1840, the mill is Cape Town's only surviving operational water mill; the cast-iron wheel was built by Jacob Letterstedt in the same year the mill started operation. Today, the Josephine Mill is the headquarters of the Cape Town Historical Society, but continues to produce the flour for which it was originally built. Visitors can purchase flour ground on the premises and, of course, baked goods. Open to the public throughout the year, the Josephine Mill and its tea garden are popular venues for summertime concerts. Because of its lush and serene setting, it is also a much-favoured venue for intimate wedding receptions.

Boundary Road is also home to the **Rugby Museum** – one of the oldest of its kind in the world – which houses a valuable collection of rugby souvenirs and collectibles dating as far back as 1891. More contemporary sporting shrines are the Newlands rugby grounds (also on Boundary Road) and the cricket grounds on Campground Road. As the headquarters of Western Province Rugby and the Western Province Cricket Club respectively, they are the setting for international rugby and cricket test matches.

Along Main Road towards Claremont, visitors will see – and likely smell the fermenting hops – the premises of **South African Breweries**, one of the country's largest and most successful business enterprises. Just a little further, in Colinton Road (off Main Road) is the majestic **Vineyard Hotel**. Built in the last year of the 18th century and imbued with all the

---

ABOVE *Sprawled across the slopes of the mountain lie the ivy-bedecked landmark buildings of the University of Cape Town.*

OPPOSITE *Approximately 22 000 students per year choose the esteemed University of Cape Town as their seat of learning.*

elegance of the period, this gracious structure was christened 'Paradise' by its initial owners, Lord Andrew Barnard and his wife Lady Anne – who acted as the official hostess at the Cape during the absence of the wife of the governor, Earl Macartney, governor of the Cape from 1796 to 1798.

Claremont

Covering what was once the Weltevreden Estate, the suburb of **Claremont** is a place of contrasts. The leafy streets are clearly the domain of the wealthy, yet along Main Road the pavements teem with informal street vendors, and impromptu stalls sprawl across the pavements. But the suburb is also home to **Cavendish Square**, one of the country's finest and most exclusive shopping complexes. The plush interior of Cavendish Square comprises up-market boutiques, restaurants and cinemas. Adjacent to the complex are equally sophisticated stores in **Cavendish Close** and **Cavendish Connect**.

For a pleasant break from shopping, take a stroll through Claremont's **Arderne Gardens**, the Victorian park laid out by Ralph Henry Arderne in 1845, situated on Main Road. The green oasis along the main artery of

the suburbs offers a chance to rest and relax. Arderne Gardens boasts not only a variety of indigenous and exotic flora, but also a tranquil formal garden laid out in Japanese style. These gardens are particularly popular with wedding parties, who compete for space to take their special photographs in the shade of the cypress, cedar and pine trees.

Kenilworth and Wynberg

To the south of Claremont is **Kenilworth**, home to the Kenilworth Racecourse and venue for the J&B Metropolitan Handicap, one of the most prestigious horse races on the sport and social calendar. Beyond Kenilworth, though, is **Wynberg**, located on a hill that was once part of Van Riebeeck's original farm Bosch Heuwel. Because it was planted with vines to serve as the governor's personal vineyard, it became known as Wynberg, or 'wine mountain'. Once a tranquil village, Wynberg is now a bustling modern suburb and its principal thoroughfare is lined with shops and large department stores. Wynberg is noted for its old Victorian cottages – particularly in the neighbourhood known as **Little Chelsea** – many of which have been re-zoned for commercial use.

Constantia & The Southern Suburbs

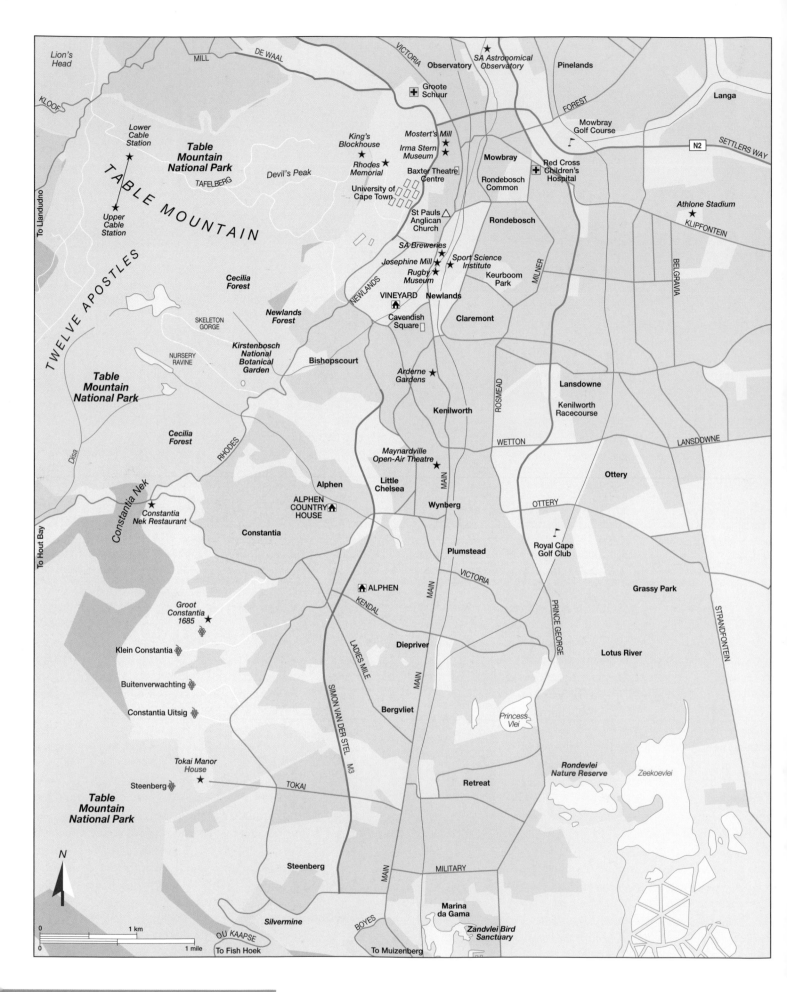

Lion's Head

MILL
DE WAAL

VICTORIA

Observatory ★

SA Astronomical ★
Observatory

Pinelands

Langa

KLOOF

Lower
Cable
Station

Table
Mountain
National Park

Devil's Peak

★ Groote
Schuur

FOREST

Mowbray
Golf Course

N2

SETTLERS WAY

To Llandudno

TABLE MOUNTAIN

TAFELBERG

King's
Blockhouse ★

Mostert's Mill ★

Irma Stern ★
Museum ★

Mowbray

Red Cross
Children's
Hospital

Athlone Stadium ★

Upper Cable
Station ★

Rhodes ★
Memorial

Baxter Theatre
Centre

Rondebosch
Common

KLIPFONTEIN

University of
Cape Town

St Pauls △
Anglican
Church

Rondebosch

BELGRAVIA

TWELVE APOSTLES

Cecilia
Forest

SKELETON
GORGE

Newlands
Forest

NEWLANDS

SA Breweries ★
Josephine Mill ★
Rugby ★
Museum

Sport Science ★
Institute

MILNER

Keurboom
Park

Table
Mountain
National Park

NURSERY
RAVINE

Kirstenbosch
National
Botanical
Garden

Bishopscourt

VINEYARD ⌂

Cavendish
Square ⌂

Newlands

Claremont

DISA

RHODES

Cecilia
Forest

Arderne ★
Gardens

ROSMEAD

Lansdowne

Kenilworth

Kenilworth
Racecourse

To Hout Bay

Constantia Nek

Constantia Nek ★
Restaurant

Alphen

Maynardville
Open-Air Theatre ★

Little
Chelsea

WETTON

MAIN

LANSDOWNE

ALPHEN
COUNTRY
HOUSE ⌂

Wynberg

OTTERY

Ottery

Constantia

Plumstead

Royal Cape ♪
Golf Club

PRINCE GEORGE

STRANDFONTEIN

Groot
Constantia
1685 ★

⌂ ALPHEN

KENDAL

VICTORIA

Grassy Park

Klein Constantia ⚲

Diepriver

Lotus River

Buitenverwachting ⚲

LADIES MILE

MAIN

Constantia Uitsig ⚲

SIMON VAN DER STEL M3

Bergvliet

Princess
Vlei

Tokai Manor
House ★

Steenberg ⚲ ★

TOKAI

Retreat

Rondevlei
Nature Reserve

Zeekoevlei

Table
Mountain
National Park

N

Steenberg

MAIN

MILITARY

0   1 km

Silvermine

OU KAAPSE

To Fish Hoek

BOYES

To Muizenberg

Marina
da Gama

Zandvlei Bird
Sanctuary

0   1 mile

Wynberg's greatest treasure must surely be the **Maynardville Open-Air Theatre**, which presents Shakespearean productions during the balmy summer months. Theatregoers may enjoy the works of the Bard under the still night sky, and picnic on the sprawling lawns beside the small lake before the performance. Reservations may be made through Computicket. Along–side the theatre, on an expanse of ground known simply as Maynardville, the representatives of charity organisations gather annually in February to host the **Community Chest Carnival**. The proceeds of the three-day event are awarded to deserving charities, and thousands of Capetonians flock to the grounds to wander amid the stalls representing the nations of the world.

Winelands of the Peninsula

South Africa is known the world over for its fine wines, but most of the Cape's wineries lie some distance inland of Cape Town. The exceptions are, of course, the vineyards across the hills and vales of **Constantia** – where the country's very first vines were planted. The valleys of this prestigious residential area are lush with woods and parklands. The hills and forest glades abound with flora, making Constantia popular among hikers and horse riders. Access to the Constantia winelands is

via either Constantia Road from Wynberg or Rhodes Drive from Kirstenbosch National Botanical Garden. The latter road is also a favourite for those who wish to take in the lavish exteriors of the homes of the rich and famous.

Constantia's Wine Estates

Travelling from Wynberg on Constantia Road, visitors first encounter the **Alphen Estate**, which dates back to 1714. Unfortunately, wine is no longer produced here, although it is distributed under the Alphen label. The first owner, Willem Adriaan van der Stel, did not incorporate the Alphen lands into his personal estate, and so the vineyards were granted to Theunis van Schalkwyk. Nearly 35 years later, in 1748, Abraham Lever erected the Georgian manor house which is today the Alphen Hotel. The grounds of the original estate are now home to the Alphen Country House Hotel and the luxurious New Court at Alphen, an upmarket housing development for the well-to-do.

ABOVE *The rural tranquillity of the Constantia Valley belies its proximity to the city centre.*

97

Steenberg, the oldest farm in the area, lies on the mountain slopes at the southern end of the valley. Located on the corner of Steenberg and Tokai roads, the farm was granted by Simon van der Stel to Catharina Ras in 1688. The homestead was erected by Frederick Rossouw in 1695. In 1990, the land was purchased by a mining company, Johannesburg Consolidated Investments. An exclusive golf club and housing complex has been laid out and investors are intent on recreating the once prominent wine estate. Fine wines continue to be made here, and the winery is open to the visiting public for both tours and tastings. The estate's restaurant, Catharina's, is also rapidly becoming as highly regarded as some of the other famed eateries in the area, notably those at **Buitenverwachting** and **Constantia Uitsig**. The stylish interior, Cape Dutch architecture and fine cuisine make for an outstanding dining experience.

Although not devoted to wine-making, the **Tokai Manor House** on Tokai Road is worth a visit, if only to see a superb example of period architecture. The mansion, with its Thibault-designed facade and traditional *stoep*, or verandah, was built by Andries Teubes in 1795. Having fallen into decay over the years, it has recently seen some refurbishment.

Situated some distance to the north, on the slopes of the Constantiaberg, is **Buitenverwachting** ('beyond expectations'). The name is fitting, for the estate is home to one of the very best of the city's restaurants, and boasts an outstanding menu of Cape cuisine. The gabled homestead, along with its cellars and original werf, have all been faithfully restored, and the estate today produces an excellent selection of wines. Although tours of the prized cellars are exclusively by appointment, the wine tasting facility allows visitors to sample all available wines. Buitenverwachting also hosts summer concerts, and is particularly known for its popular jazz recitals. Picnickers are advised to book their baskets well in advance as the service is much in demand.

Located on the Spaanschemat River Road, and adjacent to Buitenverwachting, is the **Constantia Uitsig** farm, also noted

for fine dining. Set among the vineyards of the horse-loving set, the Uitsig manor was originally the accommodation for the estate's horses, but today the stables have been converted into a graceful hotel, with both a cricket pavilion and a superb restaurant.

Tours of the 200-year-old **Klein Constantia** estate nearby are by appointment only, but for visitors keen to sample some of the best of the Cape wines, it is certainly worth the effort. The homestead remains faithful to its historic past, and there are a number of interesting diversions. Within the grounds of Klein Constantia stands a *kramat*, or Muslim shrine, dedicated to one of the last sultans (Sheikh Abduraghman Matebe) banished to the colony from Malacca by the Dutch in the late 1660s.

Constantia

In Constantia proper and within walking distance of the Groot Constantia estate is a small collection of delightful eateries and boutique outlets, selling designer homeware and other up-market bric-a-brac. Informal traders sit on the roadside touting paintings, as well as lovely, woven baskets and outdoor furniture. There is quite a selection of good eateries set amid the towering oaks: the excellent Simon's at Groot Constantia, which has quickly become the main drawcard; the bistro-like Greens restaurant, a splendid location for leisurely breakfasts and light lunches, and boasting an array of homebaked goodies; and Wangthai, one of the Cape's most popular and highly regarded Thai restaurants.

Just behind the small but picturesque and tranquil little square, on the Groot Constantia Road to the left, is the wine estate originally owned by Governor Simon van der Stel. After his death in 1712, the vast tract of land was subdivided into Groot Constantia, Bergvliet and Klein Constantia. Groot Constantia was later divided yet again and a portion was renamed Klein Constantia. Because of the inevitable confusion, the small estate became known as Hoop op Constantia, and it is still known as such today.

Groot Constantia

The ground on which the suburb of Constantia now stands was presented to Governor Simon van der Stel by Commissioner van Rhede in 1685. Magnificent Groot Constantia boasts the

OPPOSITE TOP *Charming Constantia Uitsig is the home of a renowned restaurant.*

OPPOSITE BOTTOM *The vineyards of Groot Constantia are among the few on the peninsula that continue to produce wine.*

ABOVE *Faithful to its historic past, the grand old Groot Constantia manor house symbolises Constantia's wine-making heritage.*

99

country's oldest manor house, with a vineyard that was planted by Van der Stel in 1685 – the same year the mansion was erected. In 1778, the gabled and thatched mansion passed into the hands of the Cloete family, the country's most prominent vintners. Patriarch Hendrick Cloete commissioned architect Louis Thibault and master sculptor Anton Anreith to conduct renovations, among them the addition of a two-storey cellar and a pediment sculpted with Greek gods and cherubs.

Thibault's cellar today serves as a wine museum, while the traditional high-ceilinged rooms of the manor house itself – restored after it was destroyed by fire in 1925 – houses a choice collection of period furniture and objets d'art. The nearby Jonkershuis, traditional home of the family's eldest son destined to inherit the estate, is a great al fresco dining experience. The estate's modern wine-making operation offers both tours and tastings. There is also an intimate gallery of contemporary art and a busy souvenir shop.

Simon's Restaurant is a relaxed eatery serving excellent local fare and even picnic lunches under the timber beams of the barn-like interior or under the sunny Cape skies. The surrounding grounds offer splendid views of the winelands, and are ideal for the restaurant's picnic lunches – and a bottle of the estate wine.

Constantia Nek

At the summit of Constantia Nek – the pass that links Constantia with Hout Bay – stands the 70-year-old **Constantia Nek Restaurant**, one of Cape Town's oldest eateries. With its gabled exterior and panelled interior, the Constantia Nek Restaurant remains a favourite spot for diners – the huge hearth is particularly cosy on winter evenings. On the verge outside, you may want to purchase an original watercolour depicting scenes of the peninsula.

Rondevlei Nature Reserve

Although not officially part of the Southern Suburbs, the **Rondevlei Nature Reserve** is nevertheless one of the city's most

USEFUL INFORMATION

Alphen Country House: Alphen Dr., Constantia; www.alphen.co.za

Baxter Theatre Centre: Main Rd, Rosebank; tel: 021 685-7880; www.baxter.co.za

Buitenverwachting: Klein Constantia Rd, Constantia; open 9am–5pm Mon–Fri, 10am–3pm Sat; tel: 021 794-5190; www.buitenverwachting.co.za

Constantia Uitsig: Spaanschemat River Rd, Constantia; tel: 021 794-6500; www.uitsig.co.za

Groot Constantia: Groot Constantia Rd, Constantia; open 9am–5pm daily; tel: 021 794-5128; www.grootconstantia.co.za

Irma Stern Museum: Cecil Rd, Rosebank; open 10am–5pm Tues–Sat; tel: 021 685-5686; www.irmastern.co.za

Josephine Mill Museum: Boundary Rd, Newlands; open 9am–4pm Mon–Fri; tel: 021 686-4939

Klein Constantia: Spaanschemat River Rd, Constantia; open 9am–5pm Mon–Fri, 9am–1pm Sat; tel: 021 794-5188; www.kleinconstantia.com

Maynardville Open-Air Theatre: cnr Church/Wolfe St, Wynberg; tel: 021 410-9800; www.maynardville.co.za

Mostert's Mill: Rhodes Dr., Rondebosch; open 9am–3pm daily

Rhodes Memorial: Rhodes Dr., Rondebosch; open 7am–6pm daily; tel: 021 689-4441

Rhodes Memorial Restaurant: Rhodes Memorial, Rhodes Dr., Rondebosch; open 9am–5pm daily; tel: 021 689-9151

Rondevlei Nature Reserve: Perth Rd, Grassy Park; open 7.30am–4pm daily; tel: 021 706-2404; www.rondevlei.co.za

Rugby Museum: Boundary Rd, Newlands; open 8am–4.30pm Mon–Thur, 8am–4pm Fri; tel: 021 685-3038

South African Astronomical Observatory: Liesbeek Parkway, Observatory; open 8am–4.30pm Mon–Fri; tel: 021 447-0025; www.saao.ac.za

South African Breweries: Boundary Rd, Newlands; tel: 021 658-7386

Steenberg Golf Estate: cnr Steenberg/Tokai Rd, Tokai; tel: 021 713-2233 (Golf Club), tel: 021 713-1632 (Golf Shop)

The Vineyard Hotel & Spa: Colinton Rd, Newlands; tel: 021 657-4500; www.vineyard.co.za

fascinating wild areas. The reserve is located on Perth Road in Grassy Park, and boasts an enormous variety of Cape fauna, as well as lookout points, hides and viewing towers equipped with telescopes. There is even a walkway edging the waters of the lagoon. A small museum also details the history of the reserve. Rondevlei is home to about 225 species of birds, including many water birds, but is perhaps equally well known for its resident pygmy hippos. Its most famous inhabitants are the local hippos, a number of which have gone walkabout in recent years. There is generally a media frenzy when a hippo wanders off but they have all been recaptured and either returned to the Rondevlei lagoon or relocated to a reserve.

DAY
7

THE NORTHERN SUBURBS
& BEYOND

The Northern Suburbs & Beyond

Durbanville • Tyger Valley • Goodwood • Century City • Bellville • Milnerton • Blouberg

The strip of coast that extends north of the city limits is generally considered 'beach country'. Host to a wide expanse of delicate fynbos species and vast, empty stretches of dune wilderness, it remains surprisingly underdeveloped – at least in comparison to other, equally picturesque coastal regions of the Cape. The beaches here are generally safe, with a modicum of public amenities, which makes them rather less congested than the shores that line the peninsula itself. That said, however, the stretch from Milnerton to Melkbosstrand can be quite windy at times, when the beaches are even more deserted than is normal. At the same time, though, this is also the attraction. The apparent isolation from vast hordes of holidaymakers, the gloriously sunny beach and the fact that the wind sometimes howls right down the coast, whipping up the waves of the Atlantic, make it the favoured playground of plenty of watersport enthusiasts, windsurfers, boardsailors and kite-flyers who stream here when conditions are good. In the same breath, however, the long sandy stretches can indeed get busy over the Christmas holiday season, especially now that the Cape's property boom has meant that more and more South Africans are looking at the potential of coastal real estate north of the city.

Durbanville

Inland, amid the hills of the hinterland beyond the immediate confines of Cape Town proper, is a wide region that until recently was sorely neglected by the local hospitality industry and was largely overlooked by the tourist market. This is broadly referred to as the Tygerberg Hills and, like many of the settlements along this northern shoreline, it is a boom area that has seen plenty of development. Today, the focal point is Durbanville, one of the fastest-growing towns in the country, and one that boasts not only an array of hotels and restaurants, but also an impressive number of excellent vineyards that now make up the most recent addition to the Cape Winelands. Showcase of the area's vineyards is the acclaimed Durbanville Hills Winery, an enterprise that has emerged as one of the leaders in local viticulture. Other must-see estates include Meerendal and Altydgedacht, and the olive-producing

PREVIOUS PAGES *Milnerton Lagoon is aglow in the fading evening light as the city sparkles beyond.*

INSET *Children come to grips with a python at Ratanga Junction's snake park – just one of its many attractions.*

ABOVE *The wines of estates such as Durbanville Hills Winery have rapidly earned an enviable reputation for quality.*

OPPOSITE *The tranquil vineyards and olive orchards of the Durbanville hills are a stone's throw away from the bustling city.*

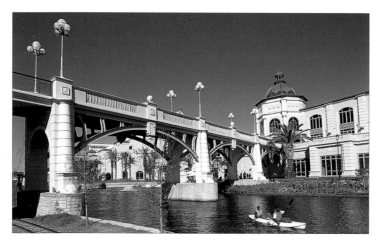

Top *Beautifully lit at night, Canal Walk shopping mall resembles a lake-side palace.*

Centre *Canal Walk's elegant interior ensures an exhilarating shopping experience.*

Bottom *Boating offers an intersting diversion for Canal Walk's weary shoppers.*

Opposite *Enjoy lunch alfresco at a Canal Walk restaurant.*

Hillcrest in the Durbanville Winelands. Notable restaurants include Poplars and Bloemendal, both conveniently situated among the vineyards.

The residential area is generally up-market, with homes fetching handsome prices on the property market, and the local infrastructure is fairly well developed. The broader Tygerberg region boasts Tygerberg Hospital, one of the largest hospitals in the country, the massive **Tyger Valley Shopping Centre** and even the **Tygerberg Zoo**, the only remaining such facility in the Cape and a favourite of youngsters. The region is popular among the younger set, with its main thoroughfare, Durban Road, lined with restaurants and bars. **Tyger Valley Marina** – a complex of up-market residential apartments, restaurants and bars – also draws the crowds.

Goodwood

Because this is where many horse studs were established in the early days of the settlement, the suburb of Goodwood – with what was once abundant green pastures – takes its name from the renowned British racetrack. But things have changed in Goodwood since then. Nowadays, it is best known as the prime location of the Cape's most famous leisure and entertainment complex, the opulent **GrandWest Casino** and hotel complex. The complex, with its towering parapets and grand architecture, is one of the most ambitious of its kind in the country. It has something to offer both young and old, and it houses in its themed interior not only an excellent ice-skating rink – both for the public and as host for local ice-hockey tournaments – but also plenty of acclaimed restaurants, bars, entertainment and cabaret venues.

Nearby is the **Northgate Island** leisure and lifestyle shopping complex and **Century City**, a massive and ever-growing business park complex that is the seat of a number of corporate headquarters (all variously styled architectural gems), and a series of impressive new housing projects that have helped elevate these outlying regions to sought-after real estate. Also part of the extensive complex is the mammoth **Canal Walk** shopping mall, which covers hundreds of hectares and is now one of the most-visited shopping complexes in the southern hemisphere. The centre itself boasts branches of most of South Africa's top retail outlets and chain stores, as well as what seems like hundreds of more specialised shops, selling jewellery and crafts, fast food and curios, novelties and gifts. The food court and entertainment arcade can become extemely busy and noisy over weekends and on public holidays, but add considerably to the vibey atmosphere of this cavernous complex.

Fairly close by is the **Ratanga Junction** theme park, home to the hair-raising Cobra rollercoaster, stomach-churning Congo Queen and Slingshot. The theme park is generally only open during the school holidays four times a year, although the corporate venues and function facilities operate year round. Alongside the park is the expansive state-of-the-art Virgin Active gym complex.

Bellville

Although Bellville – named for Charles Bell, Surveyor General of the Cape in the mid-1800s – has little to offer in comparison to the surrounding suburbs, it is nevertheless an important satellite of Cape Town. It is here that a number of high-profile corporations and industrial giants have their headquarters, and where even smaller enterprises have gravitated following the giant leap in rent and shortage of premises within the city itself.

Today, Bellville's greatest claim to fame is the **Bellville Velodrome**, a cavernous sports, retail and entertainment venue that boasts not only one of South Africa's finest indoor cycling tracks, but also plays host to big-name entertainers and international music acts, including Avril Lavigne, REM, Katie Melua, Westlife and Sarah Brightman. Adjacent to the Velodrome is the giant **Tyger Valley Shopping Centre**, which has been hailed as one of the largest, most modern shopping and entertainment areas in the southern hemisphere. Like its counterpart at Canal Walk, it is indeed huge, its acreage home to hundreds of stores, restaurants, fast-food outlets and cinemas.

Milnerton

The suburb of Milnerton – until recently known largely for its racecourse, golf course and lagoon – has its origins in an ambitious drive to move Capetonians from the security of city living and to broaden the scope of Cape Town. Early developers clearly saw more to Milnerton than the surrounding wetlands, and in 1908 – labelling the area 'Milnerton the Magnificent' – set about establishing an 'adventurer's paradise', with sailing regattas and other water sports, as well as regular attractions such as concerts featuring military bands, rugby fields and even a racecourse.

ABOVE *GrandWest Casino's cavern of entertainment caters to adults and children alike.*

LEFT *Water-soaked friends shriek with delight as they swoosh down the popular Monkey Falls ride at Ratanga Junction.*

OPPOSITE TOP *Thrilling rides await the fearless and daring.*

Despite all the hype around the fledgling settlement, the area simply failed to draw the great numbers anticipated and, while some did indeed take up the challenge to tame the great marsh lands to the north, Milnerton did not take off as the great outdoor mecca most had anticipated it would become. It even suffered some decline in the years preceding World War I, when a large part of the suburb accommodated military troops. Then, some 25 years later, during World War II, it continued the tradition by hosting regular military training exercises. Later on, just beyond its immediate borders, at Ysterplaat, an aviation unit was established. There was thus little attraction to an area that had to all intents and purposes become a rather sad little outpost, not quite meeting expectations.

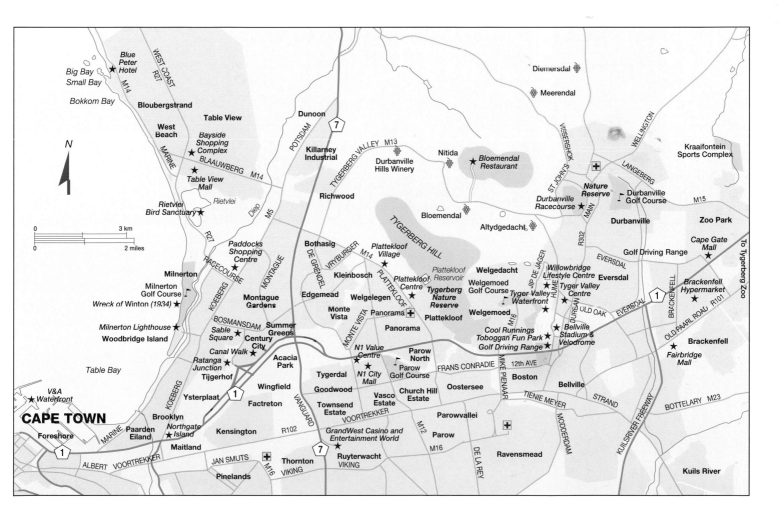

Fortunately, however, the situation began to change when Cape Town started to expand and property prices began to rocket. Ordinary South Africans soon realised what potenial lay on their doorstep and slowly began to trickle northward in search of bigger erfs, better views and lots of scope for development. As a result, things have indeed changed since the launch of 'Milnerton the Magnificent' and 'outlying' areas – Milnerton, Tygerberg, Durbanville, Table View, Blouberg and Melkbos –

LEFT *Crowds spill out onto the lawns at the Blue Peter Hotel.*

ABOVE *Milnerton golf course – between lagoon and sea – is a perfect setting for a round of golf.*

USEFUL INFORMATION

Altydgedacht Wine Estate: Tyger Valley Rd, Tyger Valley; tel: 021 976-1295; www.altydgedacht.co.za

Bellville Velodrome: Cronje Dr., Bellville; tel: 021 949-7450

Bloemendal Wine Estate: M13 off Tyger Valley Rd, Tyger Valley; tel: 021 976-2682; www.bloemendalwines.co.za

Blue Peter Hotel: Popham St, Bloubergstrand; tel: 021 554-1956; www.bluepeter.co.za

Canal Walk Shopping Centre: Century Blvd, Century City; tel: 021 555-4444 (info line), 021 529-9600 (centre management), 021 555-3600 (visitors' centre), 021 529-7211 (after-hours help desk)

Cape Town Tourism: Willowbridge Lifestyle Centre, Carl Cronje Dr., Tyger Valley; tel: 021 915-4080

Diemersdal Wine Estate: Koeberg Rd, Durbanville; tel: 021 976-3361; www.diemersdalwine.co.za

Durbanville Hills Winery: Nadekaap Wagen Rd, Durbanville; tel: 021 558-1300; www.durbanvillehills.co.za

GrandWest Casino: Vanguard Dr., Goodwood; tel: 021 505-7777

Hillcrest Wine Estate: M13 off Tyger Valley Rd, Durbanville; tel: 021 975-2346; www.hillcrestfarm.co.za

Milnerton Aquatic Club: tel: 021 557-7090

Milnerton Bowling Club: Bridge Rd, Milnerton; tel: 021 551-6452

Milnerton Canoe Club: Bridge Rd, Milnerton; tel: 021 551-9522

Milnerton Golf Club: Bridge Rd, Milnerton; milmem@xsinet.co.za; tel: 021 552-1047

Milnerton Riding Club: Koeberg Rd, Killarney; tel: 021 557-3032

Milnerton Rugby and Football Club: Theo Marais Park; tel: 021 552-5184

Milnerton Sports Club: Koeberg Rd; tel: 021 552-5152

Northgate Island: Northgate Estate, Paarden Eiland; tel: 021 511-4808; www.northgateisland.co.za

Virgin Active: Century Blvd, Century City; tel: 021 552-9045; www.virginactive.co.za

Willowbridge Lifestyle Centre: Carl Cronje Dr., Tyger Valley; tel: 021 914-7218

are beginning to take off, with some suburbs growing at an alarming rate. This, of course, means that development is fairly common here, and shopping centres, leisure facilities and hotels are springing up.

The banks of the Diep River form a small peninsula that is the setting for the housing development that is **Woodbridge Island**, as well as the highly rated Milnerton Golf Club, with its impressive golf course. In fact, the suburb's founding fathers, determined to establish a sporting heritage here, would be proud of the area's sporting record. The lagoon boasts numerous watersports clubs – the Milnerton Aquatic Club being the first port of call – while landlubbers can find their niche by contacting the local bowling, rugby, football, and sports clubs, or the Milnerton Equestrian School and Milnerton Riding Club.

Bloubergstrand

Once known almost exclusively as the site of the historic battle between Boer and Brit that resulted in the Second British Occupation of the Cape in 1806, Bloubergstrand has grown enormously in recent years. Today, the 'town' has a very youthful atmosphere, with many popular restaurants and bars lining the street just beyond the beach, while on weekends informal traders peddle their wares on the promenade. Blouberg is, however, most famous for its fynbos-lined coastline, its magical views of beach and ocean, and the landmark **Blue Peter Hotel**, which is nestled right on the beach. In fact, it is its seemingly endless beach that is perhaps its most widely recognised landmark, lying as it does at the foot of the camera frame showing a turquoise blue sea underlining the most famous view of flat-topped Table Mountain on the other side of the bay.

EXCURSION

1

STELLENBOSCH

STELLENBOSCH

Dorp Street • Die Braack • Ryneveld Street • Delheim • Morgenhof
Neethlingshof • Rust-en-Vrede • Simonsig • Spier

A visit to the Fairest Cape is incomplete without an excursion to some of the surrounding communities and wine estates. Of the three wine 'routes', or districts, located in the vicinity of Cape Town, the best known of these centres is the university town of Stellenbosch (the other wine routes being Paarl and Franschhoek). Located 48 kilometres (30 miles) east of Cape Town, South Africa's second-oldest town is steeped in history and a proud contributor to the country's renowned wine industry.

University Town

Although it is considered the centre of the wine industry, Stellenbosch is also famous for its academic institutions. The first seminary opened its doors in 1859, and the University of Stellenbosch was established in 1918. These were later followed by the founding of a number of schools and colleges. The university is renowned for its academic excellence – South Africa's first satellite, launched into space by NASA, was built almost entirely by University of Stellenbosch postgraduates – and for having produced some of South Africa's sporting greats.

One of the most significant of these seats of education was the **Ou Hoofgebou** on Ryneveld Street. Designed in Classical style by Carl Hager – the German artist who oversaw the renovations of the Moederkerk – construction of the college began in 1879 to commemorate the town's bicentenary. It finally opened its doors in 1886 as Victoria College. The fine facade includes a pediment depicting the institution's coat of arms supported by lions, a colonnaded verandah, an ornamental balcony and impressive fanlights over the upper windows.

Dorp Street

The heart of old Stellenbosch is **Dorp Street**, the monument-lined thoroughfare punctuated by venerable oak trees and ornate Victorian townhouses. The former wagon road remains

---

PREVIOUS PAGES *With a backdrop as magnificent as the Helderberg Mountains, it is little wonder that the vineyards of Stellenbosch are acclaimed among the world's most picturesque.*

INSET *Many of the vines planted in the Stellenbosch district, such as these at Delheim estate, originate from rootstock brought to the Cape from the vineyards of France.*

ABOVE *The Lord Neethling restaurant at Neethlingshof is housed in the estate's historic homestead – the perfect setting from which to enjoy the splendour the surrounding wine farm.*

OPPOSITE *The Eastern slopes of the Bottelary Hills are home to the 300-year-old Neethlingshof wine estate as well as the lush Devon Valley vineyards.*

EXCURSION

2

PAARL

Paarl

Main Street • Le Bonheur • Mountain Nature Reserve • Backsberg • Fairview • Laborie
Nederburg • Rhebokskloof • Simonsvlei • Zandwijk

The first records of what was to become the town of Paarl date from 1668, just sixteen years after Jan van Riebeeck landed in Table Bay. The first farmers would settle along the banks of the Berg River some 30 years later. In the more than 300 years since these tentative explorations, Paarl has become one of the country's main wine-producing areas.

Paarl's name comes from the pearl-like granite mountain – one of the world's largest exposed granite domes – which rises above the town. Views from here take in the valley of the Berg River and, in the distance, Table Mountain and the Atlantic Ocean. Paarl is filled with history yet offers the finest in contemporary dining, as well as the surrounding wine estates.

Historic Town

The architecture of Paarl is quite exceptional, and the **Paarl Museum** arranges special tours which walk visitors through the most impressive examples, including Georgian, Edwardian and Cape Dutch homes. Included on the tour are the charming old thatched Strooidakkerk and Zeederberg Square on Main Street. The Paarl Museum is located in the Oude Pastorie, the original village parsonage on Main Street, and houses contemporary and old Cape artefacts such as furniture, silverware and household goods of the colonial era. The magnificent 18th-century gabled mansion offers fascinating insights into early colonial life.

La Concorde, on Main Street in South Paarl, is the headquarters of the KWV, the primary exporter of South African wines. However, the KWV Wine Emporium on Kohler Street just behind the offices, is where the co-operative winemakers' association offers sales and tastings, and hosts cellar tours and lectures where visitors may learn about the creation and appreciation of local wines. It is here, too, that visitors can buy barrels and other wine-making curios and, of

---

PREVIOUS PAGES *Bountiful flora garlands the scenic Paarl Mountain Nature Reserve.*

INSET *The gabled, Dutch-style Oude Pastorie in Main Street houses the fascinating Paarl Museum.*

ABOVE *Waterblommetjies ('water flowers') plucked from the water at Schoongezicht are used to make a rich traditional Cape stew.*

OPPOSITE TOP *The common swallowtail butterfly is among the many butterfly species to be seen at Butterfly World near Klapmuts.*

OPPOSITE BOTTOM LEFT *In typical rural style, pumpkins are dried on the rooftops of even a quaint local coffee shop.*

OPPOSITE BOTTOM RIGHT *Many of Paarl's commercial ventures have made their homes in the restored residences of yesteryear.*

course, cases of KWV's popular fortified wines. The company's **Cathedral Cellar** houses the world's largest wine vats.

In the early days of the Cape colony, wagons were the primary mode of transport and Paarl was the last stop for wagons venturing into the hinterland. The **Paarl Wagonmakers Museum** tells the fascinating story of this important local industry. Exhibits include all sorts of implements and tools used in the manufacture of the all-important wagons.

For more contemporary handmade goods, visit **Le Cott Gifts and Decor**, where you can buy household novelties such as meticulously handpainted cloths and the like. Fresh local farm produce may be found at **Bien Donné Fruit Farm**, which boasts a herb garden, farmstall and intimate restaurant and hosts the annual South African Cheese Festival in April.

For connoisseurs of country life, an evening at **Bosman's Restaurant** will surpass all expectations. Located in a traditional Cape Dutch home at the **Grande Roche Hotel** on the corner of Plantasie and Constantia roads in the middle of Paarl, Bosman's is considered by many to be the finest restaurant – at the finest hotel – in the Cape. The setting, food, hospitality and service are outstanding, and the impressive wine reflects the richness of the surrounding winelands.

Paarl is also noted for the high quality of the handicrafts that originate here, and many of the home-industry outlets – there are a few on Langenhoven Street, for example – offer a wide range for sale. Visitors may browse through the exquisite pottery and tableware on display. Another famed crafts centre is the **Ikhwezi Community Centre**, where the weavers of Bhabhathane (Xhosa for 'butterfly' and symbolising the rich colour for which they are noted) use karakul wool and mohair to fashion traditional garments, tapestries and rugs by hand.

The centre also displays and sells the work of artists from Mbekweni, a small town located on the way to Wellington. Those visitors who delight in handmade items should be sure to spend a Saturday morning at the Paarl flea market, or drop by the Art and Craft Market in Victoria Park, held on the first Saturday of every month.

Wildlife

The most popular place to view the region's wildlife at close range is the **Le Bonheur Crocodile Farm**, on the Babylonstoren Road just beyond the town limits. A network of footpaths runs between dams that hold more than 1 000 of these prehistoric-looking reptiles, ranging from young adults of about a metre long to giants of up to 5 metres (16 feet) in length. The farm's breeding programme allows for the harvesting of crocodile skins, which are used to produce fine leather products ranging from small souvenirs to quality shoes and handbags. Le Bonheur also has its own restaurant, which serves breakfasts and light lunches, and offers tours that guide visitors through the farming operations.

The bird sanctuary that stretches along the banks of the Berg River is an ideal destination for bird-watchers. The tranquil sanctuary boasts more than 130 species, including eagles, and water birds such as flamingos, maccoa ducks and the beautiful malachite kingfisher.

Apart from the **Paarl Bird Sanctuary**, there is also the **Paarl Mountain Nature Reserve**, a strikingly attractive fynbos landscape best known for the massive granite rock formations

123

resting uniquely on granite clay. The veld is covered with wild flowers, rare species of indigenous fynbos vegetation, floral gems such as orchids, and natural forest glades. The pastoral environment is ideal for hiking and climbing and there are a number of demarcated walking and driving routes – such as the Jan Phillips Mountain Drive – through some of the most inspiring vistas in the Western Cape. One of the prime attractions is the Millwater Flower Garden, which is enveloped in the colourful blooms of succulents, vygies and gazanias during the spring months – be sure to catch the Chrysanthemum Show in May. Facilities within the reserve include picnic and braai areas, and the dams offer great opportunities for fishing – black bass is especially plentiful.

The Paarl Mountain Nature Reserve has numerous walks and trails varying from the strenuous to the casual stroll. Virtually in the middle of town, however, is the **Arboretum**, a green oasis watered by the Berg River and containing more than 700 species of flora.

The Paarl Wine Route

Although not quite as popular as the more famous Stellenbosch Wine Route, the Paarl route is extraordinarily beautiful, and the vineyards of the Berg River Valley produce some excellent wines. The lush countryside is virtually covered with vines, and the many estates on the official Paarl Wine Route (which also includes the farms around the neighbouring town of Wellington) make for a relaxing and memorable tour. As well as the world-renowned KWV, the Paarl area is home to the award-winning **Nederburg** estate, the venue for a noted annual wine auction.

In celebration of the district's wine-making heritage, the first Saturday in April is dedicated to the annual **Paarl Nouveau Wine Festival**, and the first weekend in September to the

that are so typical of the region. Among the reserve's most popular amenities are its hiking and mountain-biking trails and fishing facilities, mostly for trout and bass.

Be sure to take time to stop at **Butterfly World** at Klapmuts, where magnificent wild specimens flit among the lush vegetation in the natural surrounds.

Paarl Mountain

Undoubtedly the most noticeable landmark on the slopes of Paarl Mountain is the **Taal Monument**, a trio of tall structures pointing towards the skies, which commemorate the three elements that contributed to the development of Afrikaans: the civilisation of Europe, the heritage of slaves from the East and the influence of the African continent. The site includes an amphitheatre, which serves as an entertainment venue, and picnic spots from which to admire the magnificent view over the surrounding countryside. The **Afrikaans Language Museum**, situated in Pastorie Street, prides itself on exhibitions that not only look at the history of Afrikaner culture but also on the many activities and projects revolving around Afrikaans in the modern era.

Overlooking the wide Groot Drakenstein valley, the **Paarl Mountain Nature Reserve** is an expanse of wild country

---

ABOVE *The town of Paarl is watched over by the glittering monolith of pearl-like Paarl Rock.*

RIGHT *The dimly-lit cellars of the Backsberg estate occupy a cave carved out of the local rock.*

OPPOSITE *The milk of Fairview's agile Swiss goats, at home on their manmade 'mountainside', is used to make fine cheese.*

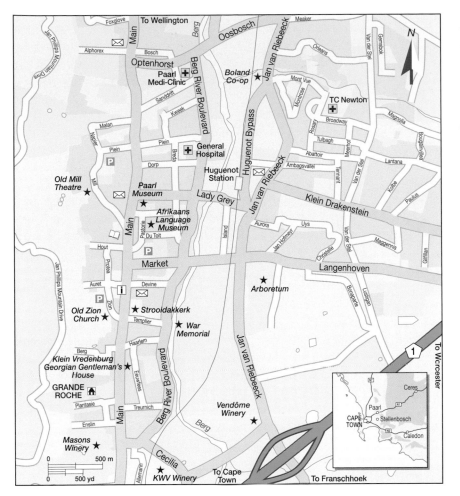

southern stretch of Paarl Mountain was bought in 1937 by Charles Back (of Backsberg fame), and is today run by a second son, Cyril, whose own son Charles is the cellarmaster. After the death of his father, Cyril concentrated on quality red wines and the estate's dry red Cinsaut is very highly acclaimed, having won a number of coveted awards. The younger Charles Back has continued in the family tradition, and is credited with introducing a fortified sweet Shiraz and being the first to make Gamay Nouveau using a unique carbonic maceration method. In 1990, Fairview also introduced a sparkling wine pressed in the *méthode champenoise* from Pinot Noir grapes. The almost purple Zinfandel produced by the estate is also quite exceptional, with a high alcohol content of 16.5 per cent.

In 1981, Fairview imported Saanen goats from Switzerland and entered the cheese market, producing feta, pecorino and other cheeses. These mountain goats are a popular attraction, and may be seen making their way up and down the custom-built staircase to their loft home. They have since been joined by milk-producing sheep imported from Germany to make the estate's Portuguese Cesa de Serra, or 'cheese of the mountains'.

Sparkling Wine Festival. Selecting which estates you will visit is an unenviable task, but be sure to taste the products of a variety of wine-makers rather than linger at just one or two farms.

Backsberg

Heralded as one of the country's finest wine producers, the **Backsberg** estate is situated on the Simonsberg. The farm was not originally planted with vines, but when Lithuanian immigrant Charles Back bought the land in 1916, he set about creating a wine estate. In 1938, he was joined by his son Sydney. The Backs concentrated on fine reds, but Sydney Back is acclaimed as the first South African producer to plant chardonnay grapes. Backsberg now also produces oak-matured brandy, but wines are still the estate's main export. Today, Backsberg is a fine establishment with its own wine museum and tours – the atmospheric cave cellar is particularly impressive – which are enhanced by state-of-the-art audio-visual equipment.

Fairview

Known for its quality wines, **Fairview** has also become famous for its cheeses. The farm on the

Laborie

Laborie, a 19th-century Cape Dutch homestead in Paarl, is owned by KWV, who transformed the estate from a fruit and table grape farm to the reputable wine estate it is today. The official name is Laborie Taillefert, after its founder, Jean Taillefert, and to honour the arrival at the Cape of the first French Huguenots in 1688. Facilities include a wine-tasting centre (converted from the original cellar), its own traditional Cape restaurant and the Laborie Guest House. Tastings and tours, however, are by arrangement only.

Nederburg

Nederburg, established more than two centuries ago, has become synonymous with fine wines. With more than 1 000 awards to its credit, it is renowned for its world-famous wine auction held annually in March. Situated in the Klein Drakenstein, the historic Cape Dutch manor was erected in 1800 by Phillipus Wolvaard. When German-born Johann Graue bought the farm in 1937, he planted the exceptional vineyards that the farm boasts today. With his son Arnold, Graue perfected a unique process whereby cold water is used to slow down the fermentation that the high temperatures common during harvest would normally speed up. Sadly, Arnold Graue died in 1953 (a year after walking away with numerous awards at the Cape Wine Show). The famed estate continues to produce some exceptional wines, among them the celebrated Edelrood in the Winemaster's Reserve Collection.

Rhebokskloof

The setting of **Rhebokskloof** is like something out of a grand historical novel. Based on the original Cape Dutch structures erected in 1692 and surrounded by a picture-book countryside, it is rural living at its best. The paddocks hold horses, Ile-de-France sheep are kept for stud purposes, the antelope after which the estate is named wander among the hills, black eagles wing overhead and black swans glide on the farm dams. Visitors looking for fine food should not miss the restaurant, as well as the convivial outdoor eatery with splendid views over the vineyards.

Simonsvlei

Simonsvlei is instantly recognisable by the giant wine bottle standing at the entrance to its cellar. In comparison to the other major wineries in the district, it was established relatively recently (1945). Its enormous variety of wines is largely due to the wide area it covers. As a co-operative (the first to be represented at the Nederburg Auction), the winemakers use grapes from areas including Klein Drakenstein, Wemmershoek, Paarlberg, Simonsberg and Muldersvlei to create the fine wines for which it has become known. Its most distinctive creations

are from the Paragon, Premier, Lifestyle and Legends ranges. The facilities include an impressive, modern visitors' centre, opened to the public in 1989. Also on the estate is a restaurant; don't miss the summer lunch in the gardens of the cellar, the wine-tasting and cellar tours. Booking is essential and tours depend largely on the season.

Zandwijk Wine Farm

Established in 1689 by Willem van Wyk, the picturesque farm on the slopes of Paarl Mountain was somewhat dilapidated when purchased in 1742 by Jacobus Bosman, who planted vineyards. When the current owners, Cape Gate (a group of Johannesburg entrepeneurs) bought the farm, it had slipped into decline and was barely viable. Without delay, they set out to prepare the vines for wine-making and to restore the farm's grand old homestead, which dates back to 1785. **Zandwijk**'s famed kosher wines are distributed under the Kleine Draken label. Vintner Leon Mostert, under the supervision of the Beth Din, travelled to Israel to study the wine-making process; all the additives in the production of Zandwijk's wines are strictly kosher. The cellars are open by appointment but are closed on the Jewish Sabbath.

OPPOSITE TOP *The vineyards of Paarl produce some of the finest wine grapes in the country.*

OPPOSITE BOTTOM *From the farmlands of Laborie estate, visitors glimpse the Afrikaans Taal Monument's towering spires.*

ABOVE *Paarl is the headquarters of the KWV, one of the giants of the South African wine industry.*

Paarl

EXCURSION

3

FRANSCHHOEK

Franschhoek

Huguenot Monument • Mont Rochelle • Bellingham • Boschendal • Chamonix
Clos Cabrière • La Motte • L'Ormarins

The tranquil valley cradling the town of Franschhoek is one of the country's most awe-inspiring landscapes, and one of its most prolific wine-producing areas. The town's name means 'French Corner', in reference to the 200 Huguenot families who fled persecution in France to settle amid the Cape mountains in 1688. They brought with them the culture and sophistication of their native land, as well as superb wine-making skills. Although the Huguenots were soon assimilated into the local culture, Franschhoek's French heritage is still discernible, especially in the fine cuisine for which the area is renowned. In July every year the town celebrates its French origins with the **Bastille Festival**, but visitors throughout the year will delight in the multitude of art galleries, antique shops and craft outlets that line its quaint streets.

Most visitors arrive in Franschhoek via the road from Stellenbosch. The other access route to the town is from the southeast via the picturesque **Franschhoek Pass**, and across the original bridge built by Jan Joubert in 1823. This is one of the oldest bridges still in use in South Africa, and offers sensational views over the valley.

Franschhoek's greatest attraction is its numerous restaurants and bistros, most of which are distinctly French in style as well as origin. The town boasts the largest number of award-winning restaurants in the country, and menus vary from French provincial to Cape Malay. Some of the finest establishments include **Le Quartier Français** (French food at its best), **La Petite Ferme** (country hospitality with dramatic views), **La Maison de Chamonix** (known for its Sunday buffet and picnics) and **Reuben's**. Most of these restaurants are within the town itself, and – unlike other wineland areas, such as Stellenbosch and Paarl – only a few of these are located on the surrounding estates.

PREVIOUS PAGES *The picnic lawns of Boschendal are blessed with towering trees, a tranquil pond and fairytale gazebo.*

INSET *Come summer, the grape harvest heralds the arrival of another memorable vintage.*

ABOVE *Forever a symbol of liberty, the Huguenot Monument remains as testimony to the town's rich French heritage.*

OPPOSITE TOP *As the home of some of the country's finest cuisine, Franschhoek boasts a multitude of restaurants and bistros.*

OPPOSITE BOTTOM LEFT *The Huguenot Memorial Museum occupies a stately house that was moved here from Cape Town.*

OPPOSITE BOTTOM RIGHT *Central to the Huguenot Monument is a figure of a woman casting off the cloak of oppression.*

The Town

The most recognisable landmark in the town is the **Huguenot Memorial Museum** and **Huguenot Monument** on Lambrecht Street, which commemorates the arrival of the French immigrants more than 250 years ago. The Huguenot Monument took 10 years to complete and was finally opened in 1948 as a symbol of the religious freedom enjoyed by the French here. The arches of the monument symbolise the Holy Trinity, while the woman carrying a Bible and a broken chain represents freedom of religion, and rejects oppression by casting off her cloak. The fleur-de-lys design on her garments reflects nobility and the globe beneath her feet symbolises freedom of spirit. The Huguenot Museum also operates as a research centre, providing information and genealogical data on the French families who settled here.

On Dirkie Uys Street is the **La Cotte Watermill**, restored to its 1779 glory with funds from the Franschhoek Vineyards Co-operative located on Main Street. Tours of the mill are by prior arrangement only, but it is worth the effort to see this fascinating piece of history. Not far away is the **La Cotte Inn**, on the corner of Louis Botha and Huguenot streets, where visitors can sample and buy the wines produced in the Franschhoek Valley.

The town is also home to a number of crafts and home industries, including **Kei Carpets**. To see examples of local art, visit the gallery on Bordeaux Street, or go to Franschhoek Vallée Tourism on Main Street.

Mont Rochelle Nature Reserve

In close proximity to both the Hawequas and Nuweberg state forests, the 1 760 hectares (4 349 acres) of the **Mont Rochelle Nature Reserve** are unspoilt and quite breathtaking, and ideal territory for walking and hiking. Trails within the reserve

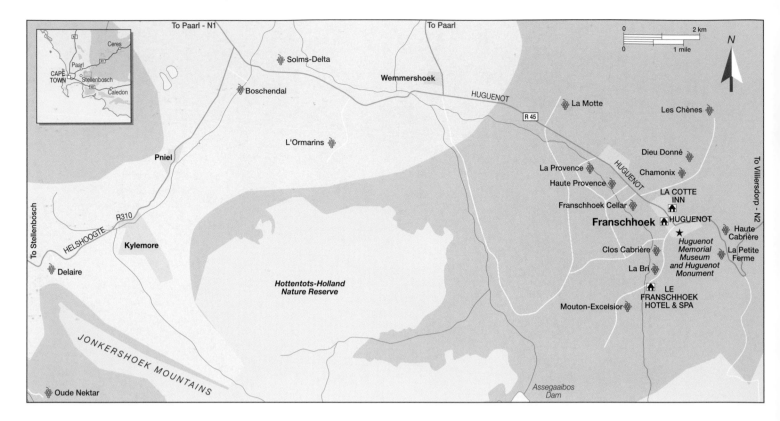

offer some scenic routes, and equally impressive is the two- to three-day Boland Hiking Trail. For information on this and other trails, contact the local municipality, the Franschhoek Museum or the Franschhoek Vallée Tourism office. Consisting largely of natural fynbos, the area covers the tracks and paths originally made by migrating wildlife – including elephants – and these very access routes were later followed by the European settlers in order to cross the rugged mountain ranges. Although open to visitors throughout the year, Mont Rochelle remains much as it was during these pioneering days and there are no recreation or accommodation facilities within the reserve. Visitors will, however, be treated to sightings of indigenous flora and fauna, among them baboon, rhebok, grysbok, klipspringer, about 30 species of reptile and the ever-present dassies.

The Franschhoek Wine Route

Established to commemorate the Huguenots and the founding vintners of the area's winelands, the **Franschhoek Wine Route** – also known as the Vignerons de Franschhoek – comprises 16 of South Africa's most distinguished wine-makers.

Estates along the scenic route include Bellingham, Boschendal, Chamonix, Clos Cabrière, Haute Provence, La Bri, La Motte, La Provence and L'Ormarins, all of which trace their origins to the Gallic settlers. However, because the vast majority of Franschhoek wines originate at the co-operative, there are few cellar tours. All are conveniently located at the Franschhoek Cellars on Main Street.

Solms-Delta

This modern incarnation of the 320-year-old Delta estate is a fine example of the development of the local wine industry so that it meets the demands not only of a discerning wine-buying market, but also those of its community. In re-establishing the vineyards and cellars, owner Mark Solms has brought the establishment into

LEFT Remnants of a bygone era are plentiful in Franschhoek, and merge well with the modern town.

OPPOSITE TOP Boschendal's renovated Cape-Flemish homestead is a tribute to the rich heritage of the region.

OPPOSITE BOTTOM Many of the exhibits in the Franschhoek Museum date back to the early days of the wine industry.

the 21st century. Solms and his team have reintroduced a range of unique viticultural practices once commonly implemented in the balmy Mediterranean climate. Today, the multifaceted farm – co-owned by the resident labourers who work the land and who have helped institute exciting new farming innovations – boasts its own restaurant (Fyndraai), museum (Museum van de Caab) and culinary gardens (Dik Delta). It is also a past supporter of the Franschhoek Literary Festival and has its own musical heritage programme (Music van de Caab); hosts summer sunset concerts and the annual Franschhoek Oesfees (Harvest Festival); and is a keen contributor to both Bastille Day and the Franschhoek Uncorked Festival.

Boschendal

The **Boschendal** estate was granted to Frenchman Jean le Long who, in turn, sold the property to fellow countryman Abraham de Villiers 30 years later. An expert vintner with a number of recommendations to his credit, De Villiers had arrived at the Cape in 1689 and was to become one of the settlement's most prominent and respected winemakers. Indeed, the family name is still highly regarded within the region's winelands, and Boschendal was one of the few estates to remain with only one owner for more than 160 years. Following the devastation of the vines by disease, the De Villiers family was compelled to sell the land in 1879 to the alternative crop farming project initiated by Cecil John Rhodes. Because fruit was less susceptible to the dangers of disease, Rhodes Fruit Farms concentrated on more varied fruit farming and began exporting the new crops to the United Kingdom. The property was finally procured by

the Anglo American Corporation in 1969. Under the professional guidance of architect Gabriel Fagan, the new proprietors restored both the farm and Cape-Flemish homestead erected by De Villiers in 1812.

The original buildings of Boschendal today house the modern developments of the estate. While the main house is the centre of the wine operation, the old Waenhuis – or wagon house – now serves as the gift and curio shop. Still standing is the Taphuis, the farm's oldest building, but a new modern winery has recently been added. Boschendal offers cellar tours, tastings and opportunities for buying wines, as well as a range of good eating venues. Not only is there a table d'hôte restaurant and light meals served by the popular Le Café, but the estate's Le Pique Nique sells packed picnic lunches during the summer months, which may be enjoyed on the lawns shaded by oak trees and umbrellas.

Chamonix

Once part of the La Cotte wine estate – one of the first to be granted to Huguenots in 1688 – the land was originally known as Waterval, but, as **Chamonix**, it has come to symbolise the best of Franschhoek. The Malan family, who took over the farm in 1947, began establishing the lands for quality grapes, and when the Pickering family purchased the property in 1965, they introduced other fruit and timber. Today, the estate – set high up in the valley and boasting its own restaurant and guest accommodation – consistently produces excellent wine

grapes. It uses the facilities of the Franschhoek Cellar to create its wines. Chamonix produced its first wines in 1983 – initially only Vin Blanc and Blanc de Rouge (now known as Blanc de Noir) – and then, in 1985, its famed Rhine Riesling. All its wines – uniquely bottled in claret bottles – may be bought and tasted on site, but visitors must make an appointment to tour the cellars.

Clos Cabrière

Cradled by mountains, this beautiful estate makes the most of its exceptional setting, carefully orchestrating the elements of sun, soil and vine to create great wines. Founded in 1694 by Pierre Jourdan and named after his home town, Cabrière estate has seen many owners make many changes to the lands. The relatively small farm currently known as **Clos Cabrière**, forming only a portion of Jourdan's original estate, is the property of the flamboyant Achim von Arnim, the highly acclaimed wine-maker at Boschendal, whose own interests lie largely in the *méthode champenoise*, by which he creates his excellent sparkling wines, using only chardonnay and pinot noir grapes. Conditions at Clos Cabrière are ideal for this type of wine, and Von Arnim has enjoyed much success with many of his wines (and those he has created for Boschendal), commanding good prices and even higher acclaim.

Franschhoek Cellar

The winery, founded in 1945 by Alberto Agostini, is based on the old La Cotte farmstead. Known for his innovative cellar methods, Agostini laid the groundwork for a fine winery. Today, however, it is also home to a wine co-operative to which members contribute their grape harvest in order to produce wines. La Cotte sells wines under its own label, and members of the co-operative operation have their own wines bottled here rather than produced under the collective name. The rest of the grapes are used to create wines that are sold to wholesalers. Franschhoek Cellar offers both tastings and sales.

La Motte

Nearly 300 years old, **La Motte** was originally the property of Pierre Joubert, but it was sold a number of times after his death until acquired by vintner Gabriel du Toit. In an ironic twist of fate, Gideon Joubert, great-grandson of Pierre, bought the farm in 1915. In commemoration of his ancestor, Joubert re-established the farmlands as vineyards and renovated the mansion, presiding over the rejuvenated La Motte for more than 40 years.

The farm was bought by the renowned Rupert family in 1970 who, in turn, restored the main house and outbuildings. The original cellar was modified to accommodate the maturation processes, and a modern cellar was opened in 1985. Although there are no tours of the cellars, it is open for wine sales and tasting. The first wines produced here were L'Etoile Légère (a low-alcohol Sauvignon Blanc) and a Blanc de Noir. The latter was created using both Shiraz and Cabernet Sauvignon.

L'Ormarins

Dating back to 1694, when it was granted to Jean Roi, **L'Ormarins** is probably one of the most beautiful estates in the Franschhoek Valley. The gabled splendour of the homestead built by later owners, the De Villiers family, looks out over a magnificent man-made lake, and the T-shaped house that is currently home to the estate manager is the oldest structure on the farm. The original 1799 wine cellar, complete with casks engraved with the coats of arms of Huguenot settlers, is now used as a store. One of the first signs of its success dates back to the 19th century when owner Izaak Marais was acclaimed for his 1833 Cape Madeira. Now owned by Antonij Rupert who bought it from his father, Anton, L'Ormarins is renowned both for its reds – among them Cabernet Sauvignon, Merlot, and Shiraz – and white wines – Sauvignon Blanc, Weisser and Cape Riesling, Chenin Blanc and Chardonnay. L'Ormarins is now part of the Anthonij Rupert operation, which includes the wines of Leopard's Creek, Terra del Capo and Protea.

OPPOSITE TOP *The views of the Franschhoek Valley from the Franschhoek Pass are unsurpassed.*

OPPOSITE BOTTOM *The Franschhoek Cellar offers a range of facilities and expertise to the region's farmers.*

ABOVE *The Franchhoek Motor Museum at L'Ormarins takes a fascinating look back at 100 years of motoring history.*

FRANSCHHOEK FESTIVALS
Franschhoek is a town known for its festivals, many of which focus on the town's other major drawcard: its food. Don't miss the following festivals in Franschhoek:
• **National Cheese Festival** (April): www.cheesefestival.co.za
• **Franschhoek Literary Festival** (May): www.flf.co.za
• **Bastille Festival** (July): www.franschhoek.co.za/bastille
• **Franschhoek Uncorked** (October): www.franschhoek.org.za
• **Spring Festival** (October): www.franschhoek.org.za

Boland Hiking Trail: tel: 021 659-3500; www.capenature.org.za
Bordeaux Street Gallery: Bordeaux St; open 9am–5pm Mon–Sat; tel: 021 876-2165; www.southafricanartists.com
Boschendal Estate: R310; open 8.30am–4.30pm daily; cellar tours; tel 021 870-4272/3/4/5; www.boschendalrestaurants.co.za
Cabrière Estate: tel: 021 876-2630; www.cabriere.co.za
Chamonix Wine Farm: Uitkyk St; open 9.30am–4pm daily; cellar tours by appointment; accommodation; tel: 021 876-2498/94
Franschhoek Cellar: Cabrière St; open 9.30am–5pm Mon–Fri, 10am–4pm Sat, 11am–3pm Sun; tel: 021 876-2086; www.franschhoek-vineyards.com
Franschhoek Vallée Tourism: 2 Main St; tel: 021 876-3603
Franchhoek Motor Museum: L'Ormarins; tel: 021 874-9000; www.fmm.co.za
Haute Cabrière Cellar: Franschhoek Pass Rd; tel: (021) 876-3688; cabriere@iafrica.com
Huguenot Memorial Museum: Lambrecht St; open 9am–5pm Mon–Sat, 2pm–5pm Sun; tel: 021 876-2532; www.museum.co.za
Kei Carpets: Main St; open 8am–5pm Mon–Fri, 9am–4pm Sat, 10.30am–4pm Sun; tel: 021 876-2192; www.keicarpets.co.za
La Cotte Inn: cnr Louis Botha/Huguenot St; open 9am–6.30pm Mon–Fri, 9am–1pm Sat; tel: 021 876-3775; www.lacotte.co.za
La Maison de Chamonix: Uitkyk St; tel 021 876-2393; tel 021 876-2393 (restaurant)
La Motte: R45; open 9am–4pm Mon–Fri, 10am–3pm Sat; tel: 021 876-3119; www.la-motte.com
La Petite Ferme: Franschhoek Pass Rd; tel: 021 876-3016
La Provence: M12, Polkadraai Rd, Stellenbosch; open 8am–5pm Mon–Fri; tel: 021 881-3858
Le Quartier Français: 16 Huguenot Rd, Franschhoek; tel: 021 876-2151; www.lequartier.co.za
L'Ormarins: tasting@lormarins.co.za; tel: 021 874-1026; www.rupertwines.co.za
Mont Rochelle Nature Reserve: Open daily; jeevee@telkomsa.net; tel: 021 876-4792
Reuben's: 11 Huguenot Rd; tel: 021 876-3772
Solms-Delta Wine Estate and Museum: Delta Road (off R45), Groot Drakenstein; open 9am–5pm daily; tel: 021 874 3937; www.solms-delta.co.za

Franschhoek

EXCURSION

4

WEST COAST &
NAMAQUALAND

WEST COAST & NAMAQUALAND

Darling • Langebaan • Cederberg • Namaqualand • Springbok

The rugged beauty of the West Coast and Namaqualand makes these regions tempting destinations for any visitor to the Cape. The West Coast extends from the suburb of Milnerton, just beyond the northern reaches of the peninsula, to the village of Velddrif, and is undoubtedly one of the country's most inspiring stretches of shoreline. The simple landscape of gentle fynbos and endless beach looks out over the waters of the Atlantic Ocean, and combines an uncomplicated lifestyle with a wealth of wildlife. But the most popular of its abundant attractions must be its spring wild flowers. Further north, the harsh beauty of Namaqualand's semi-arid wilderness is softened annually by this same miraculous abundance of spring blooms.

The West Coast forms part of what is known as the Cape Floral Kingdom, a unique biome that incorporates more than 1 000 flowering species, with no fewer than 80 plants specific to this corner of the world. Although plants vary from tubers and bulbs to legumes and herbal varieties such as buchu, the area may be divided into sandveld, renosterveld and fynbos. The most prolific vegetation type is the shrub-like fynbos, which comprises delicate ericas, reed-like restios and grand proteas. It is, however, the magnificent array of colour of the daisies, mesembryanthemums and other annuals that attracts so many visitors to the West Coast and Namaqualand every year. To keep abreast of where the finest displays are to be found, visitors can call the **Flowerline** service offered by South African Tourism. Generally, the parade of flowers is best viewed from August to mid-October, and is at its finest at around midday. Visitors should note that in order to appreciate the full glory, they should view it with the sun to their back – the flowers tend to face the rays of the sun and if you're at their back chances are you will see very little colour at all. For conservation purposes the flowers may not be picked.

An added attraction to the area is its prolific birdlife, which lures birders from all over. Naturally, the most common species are the water birds, such as flamingos, gannets and pelicans.

PREVIOUS PAGES *Stretched out along Langebaan Lagoon are carpets of the West Coast's famed wild flowers. For a few weeks in spring, the blooms provide an unforgettable parade of colour.*

INSET *In thinly populated Namaqualand, local folk still travel as they have always done, and donkey carts like this one are an occasional sight on the roads.*

ABOVE *The West Coast is home to vast colonies of gannets.*

OPPOSITE TOP *Chester the donkey is one of the colourful local characters who delight visitors staying at Club Mykonos.*

OPPOSITE BOTTOM *The splendid Postberg Nature Reserve lies within the West Coast National Park.*

Darling

The town of **Darling** in the Groenkloof district can trace its origins to 1682, when explorer Oloff Bergh first recorded the lay of the area. As the community developed, farmers began growing vegetables and grain – and even grapes – and keeping dairy cattle. The town eventually became not only a prominent wool-producing centre but also the first area in the country to breed merino sheep. Nearly 200 years after Bergh's initial visit, Lieutenant-Governor of the Cape, Charles Darling – after whom the town is now named – bought Langfontein Farm, and the popularity of Darling escalated.

The **Darling Museum** (home of Darling Tourism) concentrates largely on the influence of the local dairy industry. Exhibits here include replicas of period homes, displays on the making of butter – wooden churns and washing utensils – and a collection of period dress, furniture and farm equipment.

Naturally it is the spectacle of the flowers that lures most travellers to Darling. The third weekend of September sees the annual **Darling Wildflower Show** – coinciding with the annual **Orchid Show** at the Duckitt Nurseries – which has been prominent on the local calendar for more than 80 years. Apart from showing nearly 300 plant species, the show also provides abundant entertainment for visitors to the town. On offer are the seafood dishes and other traditional meals for which the West Coast is famous, market stalls carrying handmade goods, and even a ride on a tractor into the fields of wild flowers. It is here that the lilies, chinkerinchees and bokbaaivygies come into their full glory, interspersed seasonally with golden wheat and lush vineyards.

Not far from Darling is the town of Mamre, where it may be worthwhile to stop off at the museum at the **Mamre Mission Station**. The mission was founded by the German Moravian Missionary Society in 1808. For wine-lovers, a visit to the **Darling Cellars** on Mamreweg (Mamre Way), which is situated just 16 kilometres from the town, is certainly worth your while. The well-established cellars were opened in 1949, and offer wines of exceptional quality and value.

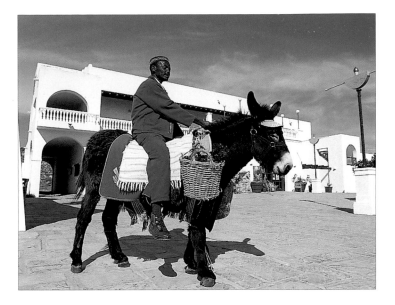

Langebaan

The 17-kilometre-long (10.5 miles) **Langebaan Lagoon**, which lies parallel to the coastline, may be considered the heart of the West Coast, and is particularly rich in birdlife. Archaeological discoveries made here include fossils dating as far back as 10 million years, and a pair of fossilised footprints made by an early human that is estimated to be 117 000 years old.

In the early days of the 20th century, the southern hemisphere's largest whaling station was established on this rugged coast. The lagoon was also the site of the world's largest oyster bed. Today, whaling has made way for gentler pastimes such as fishing, water sports and sailing as holidaymakers flock to Langebaan to escape from the frenetic city life.

The natural splendour of the region is well preserved in the **West Coast National Park**, which protects natural fynbos and one of the most impressive expanses of wetlands in the world. The original Geelbek homestead, erected in 1860, houses the national park's **Geelbek Environmental and Educational Centre**, where birding facilities include hides and a superb view over the lagoon. The park's Postberg segment provides a unique opportunity to spend two days hiking through the veld, and is also home to game and, in spring, more of the region's flowers.

August and September are both good months to see the floral displays, which include gousblom, blombos, tortoise berrybush, strandroos, sea lavender, and wild rosemary of the strandveld fynbos. There are no formal flower shows in the area, but the abundant blooms line all three entry roads into the town.

Langebaan is a centre for horse-riding, sailing, boating expeditions, rides on mules and organised overland trips in four-wheel-drive vehicles. Nearby is the Mediterranean-style resort of **Club Mykonos**. Visitors should try to sample the fresh seafood so widely available here. Undoubtedly one of the most popular eateries – so popular, in fact, that reservations are essential – is the famed **Die Strandloper** restaurant on the edge of the ocean. If you're expecting a plush setting, you're in

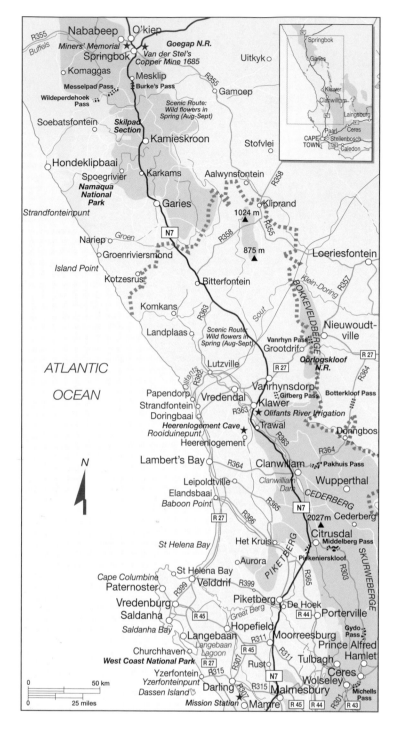

granted the original **Langrietvlei Farm** by the Dutch governor of the Cape in 1715. The 1789 manor house, filled with yellowwood and cedarwood and lit by sunlight filtering through the small-paned sash windows, is a heritage site. The farm has been presided over since 1834 by the Kotze family, who produce a unique fynbos honey, and also allow hikers and birders access to their wilderness.

The town itself boasts a row of rustic old *hartbeeshuisie* cottages constructed of clay and reeds, which are worth a visit, as is the fascinating **Fossil Museum** on Main Street. The region's fossil history is impressive: not only did Professor Ronald Singer discover Saldanha Man here in 1953, but at Elandsfontein nearby is the site of fossil discoveries that include the remains of sabre-tooth tigers, hippos and the primitive predecessors of today's horses.

Considerably more comfortable than Hopefield's original wattle-and-daub homes is the 18th-century homestead of **Kersefontein**. The farm's current owners have converted the

for a surprise. Die Strandloper is casual and rustic, and the atmosphere is decidedly relaxed. Don't be in a hurry to wolf down your meal. This is the best the West Coast has to offer, and captures the very essence of the unique setting.

Hopefield

Surrounded by open expanses of renosterveld, rietveld, sandveld and wetlands, the town of **Hopefield** is one of the most picturesque villages on the West Coast. Today, the century-and-a-half-old Dutch Reformed Church is the heart of the town, and a number of the old homes still stand. One of Hopefield's founding families was the Eksteens, who were original bakery into a cosy pub, and restored the outhouses on the edge of the Berg River into a comfortable guest chalet.

Naturally, the spring months see plenty of new blooms within the expanse of fynbos in the immediate vicinity, and the **Hopefield Fynbos Show** is held at the end of August every year. Flaming red-hot pokers, flax and erica seem to crowd the verge of the road leading from Hopefield to Velddrif.

Saldanha

The history of **Saldanha** is as old as that of Cape Town, the Mother City. The name of the town and the bay on which it stands comes from the Portuguese admiral, Antonio de Saldanha, and was first given to Table Bay – where the explorer stepped ashore in 1503. The area was home to exiled smallpox victims in the late 19th century, and has been the site of many a shipwreck. When later explorers landed at what is now Saldanha, they simply assumed that the picturesque bay mentioned by de Saldanha was where they too had laid anchor. This same bay was also the first African soil trod by the French Huguenots who settled in the Cape in 1688. More recent times, however, saw a whaling station erected at nearby Salamander Bay, and today the fishing industry is the mainstay of the economy and people of this West Coast town.

Saldanha is an expanding industrial centre, and is the site of an important deep-water harbour for the export of iron ore; tours of the facility are available. Equally important is the natural heritage of the region, which is protected by the **SAS Saldanha Nature Reserve**. The reserve itself is closed to vehicular traffic, but visitors are welcome to explore the area on foot. To view the fynbos flowers at their best, it is advisable to visit during the six-week period between mid-August and the end of September. A visit during this time is recommended if you would like to see the buttercup-like *romulea saldanhensis*, endemic to the area.

Paternoster and Beyond

Just 40 kilometres north of Saldanha on Paternoster Bay lies the village of **Paternoster**, an endearing fishing haven consisting of whitewashed cottages. This is getaway country, offering little more than casual walks on endless beaches, tranquil evenings and the freshest and tastiest crayfish on the subcontinent – the crayfish season extends from November to April. The silence and solitude here is almost divine: the name of the village is Latin for 'Our Father' and echoes the prayers of Portuguese sailors shipwrecked here.

OPPOSITE *Among the weathered outcrops within the West Coast National Park is the formation known as Finger Rock.*

TOP *The quaint Paternoster Shop serves the distinctly rustic fishing community of Paternoster, north of Saldanha Bay.*

Nearby, at **Cape Columbine**, is the last lighthouse in South Africa that is still tended by a keeper. The tall structure on Castle Rock dates back to 1936, and the Cape Columbine light was usually the first indication of land for ships approaching the southern African coast. The popular Tietiesbaai resort is located nearby, and just three kilometres (1.8 miles) from Paternoster is the **Cape Columbine Nature Reserve**. Established in 1973, the landscape of the reserve consists largely of sandveld – a combination of coastal fynbos and succulents, interspersed with rocky outcrops – which makes it an ideal habitat for birds such as the sacred ibis, as well as gulls and cormorants. The area is open to the public, and features basic camping and caravan stands, but diving for crayfish and *perlemoen* (abalone) is strictly controlled by local authorities.

Namaqualand

About 2 000 years ago, early Khoi pastoralists moved onto the land just south of the Orange River, and settled among the granite outcrops on the dry, dusty plains of this desolate area. Today, their descendants are known as the Nama, and

Namaqualand – named for these people – remains much the same as it was all those years ago, save for the growing numbers of visitors who journey here to view Namaqualand's remarkable seasonal metamorphosis. Despite the blistering arid conditions of this semi-desert, the occasional bouts of good springtime rain bring about a breathtaking transformation, covering the windy flatlands with a vibrant blanket of colourful wild flowers. The revitalised land then takes on an altogether different appearance, with springbok and mountain zebra walking the plains of the floral wonderland.

Although it is known as Namaqualand, the flowering expanse is, in fact, a series of quite small and specific botanic areas stretching northwards to the banks of the Orange River, and includes the Strandveld, the Cederberg and Olifants River Valley, the Hantam, Sandveld, Knersvlakte, Bokveld, Voor-Bushmanland, Namaqualand Klipkoppe (Hardeveld) and the majestic Richtersveld. The wide expanse of this area is world-renowned for its annual show of flowers. However, visitors may find it difficult to cover the entire region. Trips to the area need to be carefully planned to allow for overnight stays and long, tiring hours in a hot car. The villages and nature reserves closer to Cape Town offer every bit of the beauty of the region as a whole and many travellers are content to travel no further than, say, Springbok – in itself a substantial journey.

The Cederberg and Olifants River Valley

With a relatively high rainfall, the lower reaches of the Olifants River Valley boast a unique variety of plantlife (including the laurel protea and the geelmagrietjie). The fertile lands surrounding towns such as Citrusdal and Clanwilliam are speckled with fields of wheat, fruit orchards and even vineyards. At the same time, however, the less verdant lands are equally beautiful: the lower slopes feature 7-metre-tall (23-foot) waboom trees (*Protea nitida*); the rocky outcrops are home to the rare Clanwilliam cedar tree (*Widdringtonia cederbergensis*); and the valley's upper slopes feature delicate ericas and leucadendrons. Much of the area is known for its fruit, especially citrus varieties such as oranges, lemons and grapefruit – hence the name of the town of **Citrusdal**, which boasts groves of orange trees, the original seeds of which came from the Company's Garden in Cape Town. Many of the orchards in the area are open to the public, and visits may be arranged through the local co-operative.

142

Another important local industry is rooibos tea. Plantations are centred around the gracious old town of **Clanwilliam**, established in 1732. From Clanwilliam, visitors are treated to guided tours of the acres of rooibos (*Aspalathus linearis*) and the sheds where the leaves are processed, and to the flowers of the **Ramskop Wildflower Garden and Nature Reserve** and **Pakhuis Nature Reserve**, and beyond to the Biedouw Valley.

The Wilderness of the Cederberg

The **Cederberg Wilderness Area** is watched over by CapeNature, and visitors who wish to walk or hike through protected areas such as Sanddrif are required to apply for permits (available at Dwarsrivier). Plans are under way to establish the

---

ABOVE *The awe-inspiring Wolfberg Arch is but one of the magnificent rock formations one will encounter in the Cederberg Wilderness Area – hewn over millions of years by the eroding forces of wind and water.*

OPPOSITE BOTTOM *The delicate vygie is joined by innumerable spring blossoms that bring bus loads of visitors to the renowned Namaqualand region every year.*

Greater Cederberg Biodiversity Corridor, which will extend conservation plans across the entire region

Overshadowed by the 2 030-metre (6 655-foot) Sneeuberg, the famed Clanwilliam cedars of the district are not the only botanical curiosity to be found in the Cederberg: sharing the mountain wilderness are thickets of wagon trees and a rich array of flowering plants, among them pincushions, disas and other typical fynbos species; the most noted of these is the rare snow protea (*Protea cryophila* or 'cryophila', meaning 'fond of the cold'), found among the fields of snow on the upper reaches.

The action of rain, snow, water and the cold has given the Cederberg some striking rock formations. Among these are the 20-metre (66-foot) Maltese Cross, the Wolfberg Arch, Wolfberg Cracks – 30-metre (98-foot) clefts in the rockface on Dwarsrivier farm – and the Tafelberg and its Spout. Because of the many streams and waterfalls, conditions here are ideal for the formation of caves, and many of these are adorned with the rock paintings of their early inhabitants. Both the **Stadsaal Caves**, with their maze of passages and chambers, and the **Elephant Cave** at Matjiesrivier boast some fine San rock art. It is easy to understand why the San settled on this land, and why it is so popular with hikers and climbers today, as the Cederberg offers astounding views, and a variety of antelope (rhebok, grysbok, steenbok and klipspringer), cats (wild cat and caracal)

world's most prolific – begin to bloom. Through this countryside of Karoo succulents and montane fynbos flows the Doring River, which cascades over the **Nieuwoudtville Falls** to the north of the town and then over the seasonal Maaierskloof Falls. About 7 kilometres (4.5 miles) south of Nieuwoudtville lie the ancient scars left by glaciers 300 million years ago.

On the western side of the Bokkeveld mountains lies **Vanrhynsdorp**, at the foot of the Matzikama Mountains. At the end of Voortrekker Street in the town is the country's biggest succulent nursery and garden, which gives some indication of both the beauty and extent of the unusual plant forms in the area. Floral enthusiasts may choose to walk the 3-kilometre (2-mile) trail through the succulent wilderness at Kwaggaskop, about 30 kilometres (19 miles) to the north of Vanrhynsdorp. On the other side of town is a marble quarry and one of the country's most productive gypsum mines.

The harsh beauty of the region conceals many surprises. Beyond the **Gifberg Pass** – named after the multitude of hyena poison bushes that are scattered across its face – is a wonderland of protea bushes, small rivers and even a waterfall, and some fine examples of the rock paintings left behind by the original San inhabitants. From the top of the pass, you can see the green fields of rooibos tea. Where the Matzikama and Koebee mountains join, lie cultivated wheat lands and vineyards that are embellished by the springtime splendour of the wild flowers.

and other mammals such as baboons and bat-eared foxes, as well as birds ranging from the small sunbirds to majestic birds of prey such as black eagles, jackal buzzards and rock kestrels.

Over the scenic **Pakhuis Pass** from Clanwilliam, the whitewashed cottages of the Moravian Mission at **Wupperthal** preserve the timeless atmosphere of days gone by. Established in 1830, this mission settlement has changed little over the years. The simple roads still see little traffic other than the steady plod of donkeys pulling the carts of the local folk, many of whom work on the tea and tobacco plantations in the district.

The Knersvlakte

Just south of the Namaqualand Klipkoppe, the pebble-strewn hills of the **Knersvlakte** are bordered by the escarpment of the Bokkeveld and Sandveld and the towns of Bitterfontein and Vanrhynsdorp. About 50 kilometres (32 miles) from Vanrhynsdorp is **Nieuwoudtville**, set amid a semi-desert landscape seemingly covered with the fine blooms of the vygie, and annuals such as the botterblom, gousblom, nemesia and beetle daisy. To enjoy the spectacle of flowers, make a point of visiting the starkly beautiful **Oorlogskloof Nature Reserve** over the spring months. The reserve, located on Voortrekker Road about 23 kilometres (14 miles) south of the town, is inaccessible by car, and although the walk from Driefontein can be quite strenuous, the sights that await are reward enough. Baboons, dassies and bat-eared foxes scuttle among the cliffs – watch for black eagles – and the fynbos vegetation is scattered with proteas, gladioli, a variety of sugarbush and the rare *Discorea elephantipes* (or 'elephant's foot'). The Geelbekbosduif Trail also boasts at least nine San rock paintings along the way.

As the northernmost corner of the Cape Floral Kingdom, the 66-hectare (163-acre) **Nieuwoudtville Wildflower Reserve** is home to about 300 different plant species, and bursts into colour during spring when the indigenous geophytes – the

Namaqualand Klipkoppe

Separated from the shoreline by a rocky ridge, the flat plains, formed largely by the Kamiesberg and reaching from Bitterfontein to Steinkopf, are blessed with a bounty of life. Despite its name – Hardeveld means 'harsh lands' – the onset of the rainy season heralds the arrival of Namaqualand daisies and gazanias, interspersed with perdebos, kapokbos and

skilpadbos, that seem to carpet the rough valleys here. In the shadow of a crown-shaped mountain stands the town of **Kamieskroon**, the birth of which came about when the folk of nearby Bowesdorp deserted their home town – established in 1864 – in favour of a more reliable water source. Although Kamieskroon has grown since its inception in 1924, the only sign of Bowesdorp's existence is the ruins of the original church.

The region is noted for its flowers (especially impressive in August and September), and is also home to the **Namaqua National Park**. Established in 1999, the park covers an area of 138 902 hectares, which includes not only the old Skilpad reserve but also the coastal stretch around Mossel Bay. The climate is dry, but some 600 plant species have been recorded, as well as mammal species, such as gemsbok, springbok and red hartebeest. Also seen here is a variety of birds, among them the rock kestrel, black harrier and jackal buzzard, as well as plenty of reptiles. Of course, this makes the park very popular among visitors – but be warned that a reliable, up-to-date map is essential.

The hamlet of **Garies** – the original Khoi name – in the far south of the Namaqualand Klipkoppe is a small, quiet oasis known for little more than the grasses used to make mattresses, and the fact that the Garies River flows through here en route to the coast, where it empties into the sea as the Groenrivier.

Springbok

The town of **Springbok** – approximately 560 kilometres (350 miles) from Cape Town and 80 kilometres (50 miles) from the coast – began life as a mining settlement in 1685, when VOC governor Simon van der Stel began mining here, having heard of the success the Khoi people had with their primitive copper mines. The last of the shafts sunk by the Dutch governor into the face of what became known as the Koperberg may still be seen near the Goegap Nature Reserve about 3 kilometres (2 miles) from Carolusberg, while the remains of the original smelting works – dating back to the late 1600s – may be viewed at Okiep.

Although only certain sections are open to visitors, the nearby **Goegap Nature Reserve** is a paradise for hikers and naturalists. The reserve is home to aardwolf and Hartmann's mountain zebra, as well as antelope such as gemsbok, eland, klipspringer and springbok – after which the town is named. There are more than 90 species of bird, among them ground woodpeckers, dikkops and birds of prey. Facilities include picnic areas, and guided drives among the more than 500 indigenous plant species are available.

OPPOSITE TOP *The walls of the Stadsaal Caves display the artistic heritage of the Cederberg's early inhabitants.*

OPPOSITE BOTTOM *Visitors to the town of Springbok may choose to spend the night in an authentic Nama hut.*

USEFUL INFORMATION

Cape Columbine Nature Reserve: tel: 022 752-2718
Cederberg Wilderness Area: algeria@xsinet.co.za; tel: 027 482-2403 (information), 027 931-2088 (booking office)
Citrusdal Tourism Office: tel: 022 921-3210; www.citrusdal.info
Clanwilliam Tourist Office: tel: 027 482-2024; www.clanwilliam.info;
Club Mykonos Resort & Casino: tel: 022 707-7000; www.clubmykonos.co.za;
Darling Cellars: R307; open 8am–5pm Mon–Thurs, 8am–4pm Fri, 10am–2pm Sat; tel: 022 492-2276/7; www.darlingcellars.co.za
Darling Information Centre (Darling Museum): Pastorie St; open 9am–4pm Mon–Thurs, 9am–3.30pm Fri, 11am–3pm Sat–Sun; tel: 022 492-3361; www.darlingtourism.co.za
Darling Wildflower Show: tel: 022 492-3361; www.darlingwildflowers.co.za
Die Strandloper Restaurant: Jan Oelofsen St, Langebaan; tel: 022 772-2490; www.strandloper.com
Duckitt Nurseries Orchid Show: 3km from Darling on the R307; open 9am–12pm, May–Nov, first Sat of every month; tel: 022 492-2606
Flowerline (South African Tourism): tel: 083 910 1028
Goegap Nature Reserve: Office open 8am–4pm Mon–Fri; tel: 027 712-1880
Hopefield Tourism Bureau: tel: 022 723-1010
Knersvlakte (Nieuwoudtville Information Centre): tel: 027 712-8035; www.nieuwoudtville.co.za
Langebaan Tourism Bureau: tel: 022 772-1515; www.langebaaninfo.com
Mamre Mission Station: on the R307 between Atlantis and Darling; tours must be pre-arranged; tel: 021 576-1134
Namaqua National Park: Gate hours 8am–6pm daily; office open 8am–5pm Mon–Fri; tel: 027 672-1948 (Kamieskroon); www.sanparks.org
Nieuwoudtville Wildflower Reserve: Office open 8am–4pm Mon–Fri; tel: 027 218-1336; www.nieuwoudtville.com
Oorlogskloof Nature Reserve: Hike reservations open 8am–9am Mon–Fri; tel: 027 218-1010
Saldanha Tourism Bureau: tel: 022 714-4240
SAS Saldanha Nature Reserve: tel: 022 702-3523
Skilpad Wildflower Reserve: Office open 8am–4pm Mon–Fri; tel: 027 672-1948; www.africandream.com
Springbok Information Office: tel: 027 712-8035; www.northerncape.org.za
West Coast Fossil Park: R45 near Langebaanweg; open 10am–4pm Mon–Fri, 9am–12pm Sat–Sun; tel: 022 766-1606; www.museums.org.za/wcpf
West Coast National Park: Off the R27 highway north of Cape Town; opening times (April–Sept) 7am–7:30pm and (Oct–Mar) 6am–8pm; tel: 022 772-2144; www.sanparks.org
West Coast Tourism Bureau: 88 Voortrekker St, Lambert's Bay; tel: 027 432-1000; www.capewestcoast.org

West Coast & Namaqualand

SOUTHERN
CAPE COAST

SOUTHERN CAPE COAST

Strand • Gordon's Bay • Betty's Bay • Hermanus • Stanford
Arniston • Cape Agulhas • De Hoop

The southern coastline of the Western Cape is a delightful mix of cultures, attractions and unsurpassed natural splendour. Each of the communities – ranging from lively holiday resorts to sleepy little towns – along these shores has its own charm, while the waters offshore are an important whale breeding ground. At Cape Agulhas – the southernmost point of the African continent – the waters of the Indian and Atlantic oceans meet.

Strand and Gordon's Bay

Located on the eastern shores of False Bay, **Strand**'s white sands – 'strand' means 'beach' – make it ideal resort territory, and the holiday season usually sees the beaches packed with visitors. Much of this small but modern town caters for visitors, and the idyllic climate makes it that much more attractive. The Strand promenade, with its popular restaurant, juts right out into the ocean and boasts a splendid view of both the sea and the surrounding mountain. Sailboats skim the waves, children frolic on the white sand and sunbathers swim and soak up the sun. Surfers, however, tend to prefer Gordon's Bay to the southeast.

Pinpointed by the giant 'GB' marked out on the slope of the mountain, the resort town of **Gordon's Bay** has come a long way from its early days as a simple fishing harbour. Today, it boasts one of the country's finest yacht clubs and a number of impressive holiday developments, including luxurious apartments and villas, along its coast. The harbour, however, still evokes its modest past: casual fishermen cast their lines from the harbour wall or from small boats, and boats can be hired to fish the deeper waters. The two beaches in Gordon's Bay cater for the specific needs of holidaymakers. As its name suggests, Bikini Beach is the domain of sun-worshippers, while Main Beach is reserved largely for active watersports such as windsurfing, jet skiing and kitesurfing.

PREVIOUS PAGES *Backed by a rugged offshoot of the Hottentots-Holland Mountains, Clarence Drive winds along the scenic eastern shore of False Bay from Gordon's Bay to Pringle Bay.*

INSET *Undoubtedly the most thrilling of sights in spring is the breeching of southern right whales off Hermanus. The whales come here in spring to bear their young.*

ABOVE *Hermanus's official whale crier, Pieter Claasen, welcomes Maurice Jones, a town crier from Farford in the United Kingdom.*

OPPOSITE TOP *A Gordon's Bay chandler's shop manifests the town's longstanding link with the sea.*

OPPOSITE BOTTOM *Strand's beach is a magnet for sailors.*

Hangklip to Kleinmond

Initially a whaling station, the small town of **Betty's Bay** was established as a somewhat exclusive getaway spot in the 1930s. It is still a relatively quiet holiday location but, like many other villages on this coast, is particularly popular over the end-of-year holiday season as people flock to the coast.

Despite the resort atmosphere, this part of the Cape coast also caters for nature lovers. Disa Kloof at the nearby **Harold Porter National Botanical Garden** on the mountain slopes, for instance, is a natural paradise, with a magnificent stream and waterfall, and a multitude of wild flowers, including the disa. Just as enchanting is **Stony Point Reserve**, about 188 hectares

(465 acres) of mostly montane fynbos, and the first nature reserve to be declared on the southern African subcontinent. The vivid red disa is particularly prevalent over December, and the reserve is also a breeding sanctuary for African penguins. If the fynbos vegetation is of special interest, be sure not to miss out on the display at the **Kogelberg Nature Reserve**. Located near Kleinmond and about 10 kilometres (6 miles) east from Betty's Bay, Kogelberg is managed as a biosphere reserve, which ensures the protection of sensitive areas and biological diversity. The reserve, and especially its Kogelberg Trail, is most noted for its splendid show of fynbos – about 20 per cent of fynbos species are found here – but there is also plenty of small wildlife to view, including antelope, and numerous bird species.

Canoeing is permitted on the Palmiet River, which forms one of the borders of Kleinmond, a small coastal town tucked between the Palmiet and Bot rivers. The surrounding fynbos-covered mountainside is also ideal for hikers, as is the **Kleinmond Coastal Nature and Mountain Reserve**. The 1 000-hectare (2 470-acre) reserve is home to more than 1 500 indigenous plant species, including the endemic *Erica pillansii*, and also the micro frog – the world's rarest amphibian. Hiking trails cover both the confines of the reserve and the adjoining Kleinmond Lagoon.

Hermanus

During the holiday season, **Hermanus** bustles with holidaymakers, but off-peak periods are considerably more sedate. The seaside town ranks as one of the Cape's most popular getaway spots, and accommodates visitors from near and far. The relatively new harbour now houses a modern clubhouse and a variety of boats and watersport equipment, including windsurfers and surf-skis – popular pastimes along this stretch of the southern Cape coast. Sunset cruises from the harbour are a perennial favourite with holidaymakers. The accent in Hermanus is most definitely on having fun and the town is dotted with pubs, restaurants, stylish cafés and braai spots; and, of course, the beaches teem with bikini-clad bathers, surfers and sun-worshippers. The largest and most popular stretch of sand is **Grotto Beach**, which stretches past the Klein Rivier Lagoon to **Die Plaat**.

A favoured Hermanus hangout is the **clifftop path** overlooking Walker Bay, the country's top whale-watching spot. This vantage point is presided over by the world's only official **whale crier**, whose job is to alert the public – he carries a horn made of kelp – that whales have been spotted in the bay. For this purpose, he now also carries a cellphone to keep his followers abreast of the migration patterns and movements of the whales. A number of tour guides operating in the Walker Bay area offer visitors the chance to descend in underwater cages to see **great white sharks** – now a protected species in South African waters.

Because the seas off Hermanus form part of a marine reserve, divers who wish to brave the ocean either to explore or to search for seafood delicacies are obliged to purchase permits from the

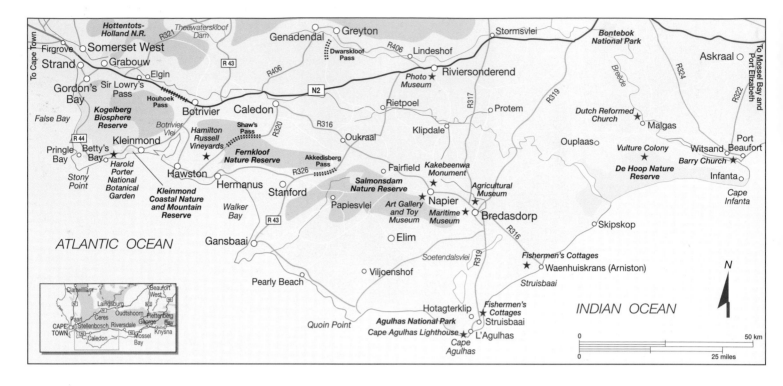

magistrate's office on Main Road. For the less adventurous, there is plenty to see on land. Apart from the seals, which tend to congregate in the area, the view from the top of the cliff overlooking the **Old Harbour** is quite spectacular.

The harbour itself offers a number of fascinating diversions. There is the **Harbour Museum**, whose exhibits tell the story of the local whaling and fishing industry. These exhibits include part of a whale skeleton and seawater tanks brimming with the plant and animal life found out to sea. For the benefit of whale-watchers, telescopes have been set up above the Old Harbour

– there are also coin-operated ones on Village Square – and sonar equipment allows visitors to hear the calls of the whales off the coast.

At the foot of the harbour cliffs stands the **Aba Gold Perlemoen Hatchery** where abalone are bred – either to be released (in order to maintain the indigenous population) or sold to the specialised abalone 'farmers' in the region. Appointments may be made to tour the operation.

Covering much of the area inland from Hermanus, the 1 550-hectare (3 830-acre) **Fernkloof Nature Reserve** stretches

from Maanskynbaai to Hemel-en-Aarde valley and boasts a 60-kilometre (37-mile) network of excellent walking trails – demarcated and colour-coded according to difficulty and length – through coastal and montane fynbos terrain. The reserve features ericas, proteas and over 1 000 other plant species (many of which may be seen on display at the visitors' centre). More than 100 bird species frequent the reserve, and mammals such as baboons and small antelope are quite common. Fernkloof's Spring Wildflower Festival usually takes place in September, at about the same time as the annual Whale Festival (the arrival of the southern right whales to their waters) a community celebration involving a variety of entertainment in a convivial atmosphere.

The people of Hermanus do not depend on the seasonal visitors, and the town has developed a number of small industries of its own. Many of the country's most prominent painters and artists live and work in and around Hermanus,

and there are numerous craft shops, galleries and flea markets where visitors can purchase locally produced items.

Because of the town's location, its many restaurants naturally emphasise local seafood. There are a number of popular eateries in and around the centre of town, many of which boast impressive views over the ocean. Topmost among these are the up-market **Pavilion at The Marine** (à la carte menu and carvery), **Kate's Village Restaurant** (country fare) and **Bientang's Cave**, which nestles in the base of the cliff overlooking the beach and is thought to be the original home of Bientang, the last indigenous Strandloper ('beach walker') of these parts. Booking at most of these venues is essential.

Wine-lovers should certainly not forget to stop at the **Bouchard Finlayson** and **Hamilton Russell Vineyards**, both

OPPOSITE *The panoramic Old Harbour of Hermanus is now a heritage site, and boasts extraordinary views of Walker Bay.*

ABOVE *The fishing village of Waenhuiskrans is also called Arniston, after a British troopship that sank here in 1815.*

RIGHT *Fishing is an important industry in and around Arniston, and local delicacies include dried fish.*

151

principle of 'women and children first'. Tours of the memorial and lighthouse may be arranged with the local Information Office.

To the south lies the aptly named **Pearly Beach**, a peaceful strip of sparkling sand popular among anglers and divers who visit Dyer Island – with its colony of penguins – just off the coast. A little further along the coast from Pearly Beach is probably the most famous spot along this shoreline: L'Agulhas and the famed **Cape Agulhas Lighthouse**, erected in 1848. Cape Agulhas is Africa's southernmost tip and the confluence of the two oceans, but it is also one of the most treacherous stretches of coast on the continent, known locally as the Graveyard of Ships. The lighthouse is open to the public and has a coffee shop and small museum.

Just beyond Agulhas is the small resort town of **Struisbaai**, a 14-kilometre (9-mile) strip of pristine beach said to be the longest in the southern hemisphere. The name of the village is taken from the many ostriches that once roamed the land here. (The Afrikaans word for ostrich is *volstruis*.) Although considered by many as lost in time, the little hamlet offers weary travellers the opportunity to catch their breath by either fishing off the rocks or taking a relaxing pleasure cruise. Virtually the entire shore is dotted with historic fishermen's cottages, which reach as far as **Arniston**. This popular retreat, with its thatched cottages and snow-white sands, was traditionally a fishing village. The quaint community was originally known as Waenhuiskrans (meaning 'wagon house cliff'), after the great cavern overlooking the beach a short walk to the southwest of the village.

set in the picturesque Hemel-en-Aarde valley on the fringe of the town. The vineyards are quite spectacular, and visitors can sample some of the estates' fine wines.

Stanford to Arniston

The little village of **Stanford**, on the banks of the Klein River, is rich in both history and rural atmosphere, and offers a more tranquil lifestyle than resort towns such as Hermanus. Here, visitors may take boats and canoes out onto the river, amble through the fynbos vegetation and watch the plentiful birdlife that inhabits the district. In fact, a favourite bird-watching spot is the nearby **Salmonsdam Nature Reserve**, where an array of bird species flit about the montane fynbos and over the breathtaking mountains and vales.

Gansbaai, on the other hand, remains a traditional fishermen's village, complete with rustic old cottages and fishing fleets. Modern progress has allowed for the development of a new harbour, and a fishing factory has also been established in the vicinity. Fortunately, these changes have not detracted from the tranquil beauty of this charming little bay, and – like Struisbaai to the east – Gansbaai is a favoured getaway for many Capetonians. The most prominent natural feature of this stretch of shoreline is the 8-kilometre (5-miles) 'peninsula' known as Danger Point. The most famous victim of this jagged coastline was HMS *Birkenhead*, a British troopship that ran aground on 26 February 1852 on the rock which has now taken its name. More than 400 men lost their lives on that fateful night, which gave rise to the Birkenhead Drill – the

De Hoop Nature Reserve

Although the **De Hoop Nature Reserve** is not accessible from Arniston (the nearest access point is at Ouplaas), to miss out on the reserve would be a pity, especially for bird-watchers. The 40-kilometre (25-mile) shoreline boasts a marine reserve extending 5 kilometres (3-mile) out into the Indian Ocean – both swimming and diving are allowed – and a 14-kilometre (9-mile) lagoon that is a drawcard for over 250 bird species. Many waders and nearly all South Africa's water birds are found here, as well as species such as the Damara tern, the Cape vulture and the black oystercatcher. A number of mammal species may also be spotted here, among them bontebok, eland, rhebok, zebra, baboon, grey mongoose, caracal and the endangered Cape clawless otter. There is a fascinating diversity of plant life – about 50 of De Hoop's 1500 plants are endemic – including the Bredasdorp sugarbush.

Watching the Whales

Although the **Western Cape Whale Route** actually starts as far away as Lambert's Bay on the West Coast, it is the southern Cape coast that is traditionally the best spot to see the whales cavorting in the ocean with their young. Because of the popularity of this natural spectacle, at least 45 special information boards have been posted at various locations along the route, providing enthusiasts with details on the visiting species and their most favoured spots.

Although the calving season may begin as early as June – the humpbacks start migrating from about May and Bryde's whales are seen virtually throughout the year, albeit further out to sea – the months between August and November will almost guarantee a sighting. Southern right whales are attracted by the warmer waters and abundance of food, and it is here that they give birth to their young and nurse them until the calves are strong enough to travel. Whale-watchers flock to the shores of Stony Point near Betty's Bay, Kleinmond, Onrus, De Kelders and Koppie Alleen in the De Hoop Nature Reserve, but viewing boats are forbidden to approach within 300 metres (915 feet) of the whales. The most popular spot to see the animals, however, is at Hermanus, the very centre of the Whale Route, and one of the best sites for whale-watching in the world.

OPPOSITE TOP *Cape Agulhas is Africa's southernmost tip, and the point where the Atlantic and Indian oceans meet.*

OPPOSITE BOTTOM *The welcoming beacon of the Cape Agulhas Lighthouse has long guided mariners past this treacherous coast.*

ABOVE *Visitor accommodation at De Hoop Nature Reserve is styled along the classic lines of local vernacular architecture.*

RIGHT *Cycling is just one way to appreciate the diversity and unspoiled environment of De Hoop.*

USEFUL INFORMATION

Aba Gold (Perlemoen Hatchery): tel: 028 313-0253; www.abagold.com

Arniston Hotel: tel 028 445-9000; www.arnistonhotel.co.za

Arniston (Waenhuiskrans) Information Centre: Open 8am–5pm Mon–Fri, 9am–12pm Sat; tel: 028 424-2584; www.capeagulhas.co.za

Cape Agulhas Information Centre (Bredasdorp): Open 8am–4pm Mon–Fri; tel: 028 424-2584

Cape Agulhas Information Centre (Hermanus): Open 8am–4pm Mon–Fri; tel: 028 312-2629

Cape Agulhas Lighthouse (Soetendalsrand Nature Reserve): Open 9am–4.30pm daily; tel: 028 435-6078; www.sanparks.org

Cape Overberg Tourism Association: Office open 8am–4.30pm Mon–Fri; tel: 028 214-1466; www.capeoverberg.org

De Hoop Nature Reserve: Gate hours 7am–6pm daily (Fridays 7am–7pm); tel: 028 542-1253 (enquiries), 021 659-3500 (reservations); www.capenature.co.za

Fernkloof Nature Reserve: Open 8am–7pm daily; tel: 028 313-8100

Gansbaai Tourism Bureau: Open 9am–5pm daily; tel: 028 384-1439; www.gansbaaiinfo.com

Hangklip/Kleinmond Tourism Bureau: tel: 028 271-5657; www.ecoscape.org.za

Harold Porter National Botanical Garden: Open 8am–4.30pm Mon–Fri, 8am–5pm Sat–Sun; tel: 028 272-9311; www.sanbi.org

Hermanus Tourism Bureau: Open 9am–5pm Mon–Sat; tel: 028 312-2629; www.hermanus.co.za

Kleinmond Coastal Nature Reserve: tel: 028 271-8100

Kogelberg Biosphere Reserve: Open daily 8am–4.30pm; tel: 028 271-5138; wwwcapenature.co.za

Stanford Information Centre: Open 8am–4pm Mon–Fri, 9am–5pm Sat, 9am–1pm Sun; tel: 028 341-0340; www.stanfordinfo.co.za

Struisbaai Information Centre (Cape Agulhas Tourism): Open 8am–4pm Mon–Fri; tel: 028 424-2584

153

EXCURSION

6

THE GARDEN ROUTE

THE GARDEN ROUTE

Mossel Bay • Oudtshoorn • George • Wilderness • Knysna
Plettenberg Bay • Tsitsikamma

The scenic splendour that is the Garden Route has been heralded as the Cape's finest treasure, and a visit to this 230-kilometre (140-mile) stretch of sparkling sands, rugged cliffs, wild flowers and sleepy inland waters will testify to this tribute. The roads that lead from Mossel Bay to the Tsitsikamma forests are shielded by the Outeniqua and Tsitsikamma mountain ranges, lined with a breathtaking array of lagoons and lakes, coves and cliffs, and lapped by the warm waters of the Indian Ocean. The Garden Route shelters a fascinating diversity of plant and animal life, and is also a leisure playground – with attractions such as water-skiing, boating, diving, paragliding, fishing, swimming and surfing.

Mossel Bay

The Garden Route starts officially at **Mossel Bay**, a small but well-established resort town 390 kilometres (240 miles) from Cape Town. Blessed with balmy summers and moderate winters, the beaches of this seaside town have long been a favoured holiday spot. For a glimpse of what the town offers, visit in June when the **Food and Wine Festival** is held.

By the time Bartolomeu Dias first visited the picturesque cove in 1488, the area we know today as Mossel Bay had already been settled by Strandlopers – a nomadic clan of Khoi who travelled the beaches of the Cape, living on what was offered by the ocean, including the mussels for which the bay is named. Mossel Bay has seen considerable development since the Portuguese explorer set foot here. The streets are lined with many heritage sites, and the town enjoys an enviable reputation for the fine seafood caught nearby. In recent years, the extraction of offshore gas and oil deposits has brought considerable development to the town. However, Mossel Bay's charm stems from its colourful history and maritime influence

---

PREVIOUS PAGES *The magnificent stretch of beach at Nature's Valley signals the end of the famed Otter Trail.*

INSET *The thriving ostrich farms of Oudtshoorn offer a fascinating diversion along the Garden Route.*

ABOVE *Mossel Bay's Bartolomeu Dias Museum chronicles more than 500 years of maritime history.*

OPPOSITE TOP *The magical qualities of the Cango Caves attract many thousands of sightseers each year.*

OPPOSITE LEFT *Girded by quiet gardens, George's Dutch Reformed Church watches over the town.*

OPPOSITE RIGHT *Mossel Bay's Dias Monument is dedicated to the Portuguese mariner who was the first European to set foot here.*

– commemorated at the annual **Dias Festival**. In 1988, to mark the 500th anniversary of the Dias expedition, the **Bartolomeu Dias Museum** was established, and its satellite museums and monuments – the Maritime Museum, Munro's Cottages and the Dias Cross – are popular drawcards. One of the most intriguing sights is the famed **Post Office Tree**, a giant old milkwood where sailors would leave letters to be collected by the next ship heading for home.

Mossel Bay is closely tied to the sea, and many visitors are drawn by its marine life. Whales and dolphins may be sighted beyond the breakers – The Point is an excellent vantage spot – and African penguins and seals may be seen right throughout the year. In fact, a number of local operators offer harbour cruises, which take sightseers and nature lovers to the shores of **Seal Island**, the home of a massive colony of nearly 2 000 seals that, on a clear day, can be seen from land.

Ostrich Country

Enclosed by the mountains of the Outeniqua and Swartberg ranges, the town of **Oudtshoorn** is the seat of the Little Karoo's

'ostrich kingdom'. Oudtshoorn is dotted with monuments and museums, including the **CP Nel Museum**, with its period furniture and ostrich mementoes, and the **Cango Caves Museum**. The town is perhaps most renowned for its 19th-century 'feather palaces' – extravagant manor houses erected by wealthy ostrich farmers at the height of the feather boom – and as the home of the magnificent **Cango Caves**, located about 30 kilometres (19 miles) north of the town. Carved by water dripping through layers of limestone rock, the spectacular chambers and dripstone formations attract thousands upon thousands of visitors every year. Consisting of a series of winding passages and soaring chambers held aloft by towering pillars, the Cango Caves are among the most impressive in the world. The largest of the caverns is Van Zyl's Hall, a mammoth chamber over 100 metres (330 feet) long, 55 metres (180 feet) wide and 17 metres (56 feet) high. There are few formations within these stone walls that do not inspire awe, including the dripstone Organ Pipes, Cleopatra's Needle and the Frozen Waterfall. Access to this important heritage site is now strictly regulated to preserve the caves in their natural state. Sadly, vandals have already left their mark, and the lights erected for better viewing have resulted in the growth of moss and algae. There are approximately 3 kilometres (2 miles) open to public exploration; visitors who take one of three-hourly tours are requested to abide by the rules.

For those who wish to see some of Africa's wildlife, a visit to the crocodile farming operation at **Cango Wildlife Ranch** is a must. Here, more than 400 alligators and crocodiles are bred for research purposes. Although criticised by animal activists for caging wild animals,

157

such as lions, cheetahs, leopards and the exotic jaguar and puma, the park-like operation is a genuine attempt to educate the public, many of whom may never have the opportunity to see these majestic creatures in their natural habitat. In fact, the ranch is the headquarters of a very successful cheetah breeding project, and visitors are invited to view and photograph the animals from the safety of a walkway running above the spacious enclosures. The farm has a popular reptile house, otter pond and pens housing pygmy hippos and a pack of endangered wild dogs. There is also a cheetah contact centre, as well as a Natural Encounters education and awareness programme that allows access to the cheetahs, a white tiger, snakes and crocodiles.

No visit to Oudtshoorn would be complete without an encounter with the birds that made the town famous. Some of the local ostrich farms – including Highgate, Safari and the Cango Ostrich Show Farms – are open to the public. Visitors may ride on the backs of these giant, flightless birds, visit the breeding stations and hatcheries, and purchase ostrich plumes, eggs, meat (including biltong), leather products and other curios. Also on offer in and around the town are forest and fynbos tours, a number of other wildlife encounter adventures (including camel rides and game-viewing), ever-popular township tours and hiking and horse-riding options.

LEFT *The breathtaking Outeniqua Pass connects George with the town of Oudtshoorn in the Little Karoo.*

OPPOSITE *The Kaaimans River Bridge between George and Knysna crosses over the Kaaimans as it winds its way to the coast.*

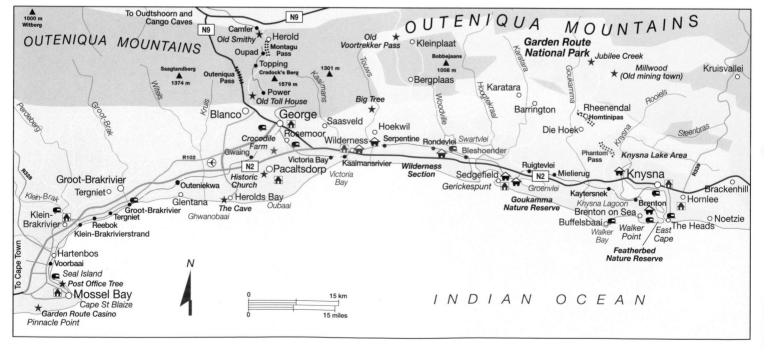

George

Named for King George III, this historic centre of the Garden Route lies in the shadow of the lush Outeniqua Mountains, surrounded by the natural glory with which the district has become synonymous. The landscape around **George** is one of bountiful rivers, prosperous farmland and colourful flora.

Together with neighbouring Heroldsbaai, Wilderness and Sedgefield, the town is an extremely popular leisure stop for anglers and watersport enthusiasts.

Housed in the town's old courthouse, the **George Museum** is an excellent place to explore local heritage – make a point of seeing the collection of old gramophones. The museum also tells

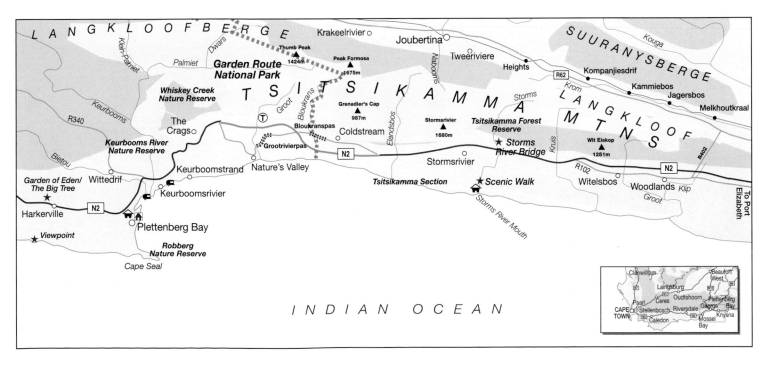

the story of the local timber industry, which is based on the indigenous forests in the vicinity. To view a selection of the fine yellowwood and stinkwood products manufactured here, be sure to visit the local factories or the outlet in York Street.

Equally important to the town's character are its many houses of worship – not for nothing was George known as Cathedral City. The most impressive features are the domed ceiling of the **Dutch Reformed Church**, the stained-glass windows of **St Mark's Cathedral**, and **St Peter and St Paul**, the oldest surviving Catholic church in South Africa.

Sporting pursuits are well catered for here. George is home not only to a number of excellent golf courses – **Fancourt Country Club** boasts a championship course – but there is also the local riding club, the George Sports Club, and a number of favourite watersport venues: safe swimming and surfing at Victoria Bay; waterskiing at Rondevlei and Swartvlei; snorkelling at Gericke's Point; bass fishing at Lake Pleasant; and numerous fishing spots stretching from Glentana through to Plettenberg Bay.

A relatively new development that is quite close to town is George's own crocodile park, a small research facility that not only breeds crocodiles, but is also home to a variety of indigenous bird species.

Wilderness

As its name suggests, the Wilderness area is precisely that – a great stretch of unspoilt terrain at the foot of the Outeniqua mountains. This is the setting for the **Wilderness section of the Garden Route National Park**, which includes Wilderness Lagoon, the Touws River estuary, the Rondevlei and Swartvlei lake system and part of Groenvlei, which forms the border with the Goukamma Nature Reserve to the west. It is bounded in the south by the Indian Ocean. This natural haven caters for nature lovers, who flock to the area: whale-watchers, horse-riders, bird-watchers (about 200 bird species may be spotted from various hides in the Wilderness section, about 80 of which are water birds) and the many sport lovers who hang-glide, parasail and hike here – especially popular is the 12-kilometre (7.5-mile) **Kingfisher Trail**.

With its spectacular natural forests and wildlife, nearby **Sedgefield** is an equally popular retreat that offers much the same sorts of diversion as Wilderness. The tranquil waters here are edged with beds of reeds and sedges – from which the town gets its name – and the wildlife, attracted by the bountiful source of food and shelter, is equally prolific. Gericke's Point, popular among spear-fishermen, boasts some fascinating rock formations, and just as interesting is the water life of Swartvlei, a saltwater lake that is ideal for swimming and other water-based leisure activities.

Adjoining the fishing paradise of Groenvlei – also known as Lake Pleasant – is the **Goukamma Nature Reserve** and the adjacent marine reserve. Goukamma incorporates just over

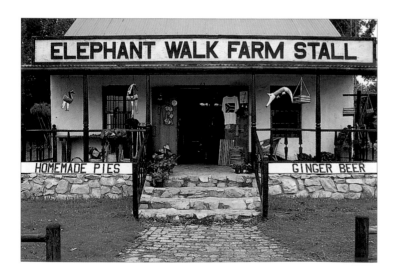

ABOVE *Wilderness National Park's rest camps offer the tranquillity suggested by the park's name.*

LEFT *Like many of the old-fashioned farmstalls of the district, Knysna's Elephant Walk Farm Stall offers homemade delicacies.*

OPPOSITE *The craggy Heads form a narrow entrance to the peaceful holiday playground of Knysna Lagoon.*

2 000 hectares (4 940 acres) of largely coastal fynbos vegetation, with a network of more than 35 kilometres (22 miles) of trails, ranging from 4-kilometre (2.5-mile) hikes (taking about 1½ hours) to 14 kilometres, or 9 miles (about 5 hours). A number of watersports are permitted, although permits are necessary to fish the waters of the reserve. The flora and fauna are important drawcards: over 200 bird species have been recorded here, and Goukamma is home to both the common and blue duiker, vervet monkeys, the Cape grysbok and bontebok. The latter is found in protected areas of both the Goukamma Nature Reserve and the Garden Route National Park. The splendour of the Wilderness lakes region, however, does not end with Sedgefield but extends much further to Buffalo Bay and Walker Point – both favourite holiday destinations – and beyond to Brenton-on-Sea.

Knysna

The 'beautiful land' – as depicted on its coat of arms – is indeed a gift of the gods. Of all the enchanting spots along the Garden Route, the finest must be the **Knysna Lake Area**, a spectacularly unspoilt expanse that includes the town of Knysna, the surrounding forests, the lagoon and the rocky Knysna Heads that guard this sanctuary. Because it is one of the country's favourite holiday and tourist destinations and situated on South Africa's biggest and most valuable estuary, the area is closely monitored by conservationists. Other reasons to safeguard the area include the over 36 000 hectares (89 000 acres) of indigenous forests, which contain mostly yellowwood and stinkwood, and Knysna Lagoon's oyster-farming operations – visit in July to sample the fresh seafood at the annual **Knysna Oyster Festival**. The area is also home to some unique species that have now become synonymous with Knysna: the pansy shell, the Knysna turaco (loerie) and the Knysna seahorse.

The town itself is part of the original property owned by George Rex, a man of mystery and legendary character who lived here in the early 1800s and is said to have been an illegitimate son of George III. None of the tales has ever been proven, but they do add to the romantic charm of the town. Today, a small yellowwood structure houses the **Knysna Museum**, which not only tells the story of Rex, but also displays the history of the modern town. The building originally stood on the site of the country's first gold diggings at **Millwood**, some 25 kilometres (16 miles) northwest of Knysna, and is currently being redeveloped to restore it to its former glory.

Although Knysna does have its fair share of modern shopping complexes and chain stores, the small characterful arts-and-crafts and home-industry outlets remain the most alluring. One such place is the **Elephant Walk Farm Stall** on the outskirts of the town, which stocks handmade crafts and freshly made pies and snacks.

The Knysna Lagoon boasts an innovative harbour precinct known as **Knysna Quays**, a waterfront development catering largely for the leisure recreation of visitors. Although colourful and vibrant, it is rather more expensive than the facilities

161

Plettenberg Bay is still one of South Africa's premier and most fashionable leisure spots. The first people to settle in the area were Portuguese sailors who were stranded here after the *São Gonçalo* foundered off the nearby coast in 1630. Ming porcelain recovered from the wreck forms part of the Jerling Collection at the town's municipal offices. A whaling operation situated on Beacon Island has now made way for an impressive hotel complex, and the lagoon and beaches crawl with holidaymakers. Central Beach is the in spot for watersport junkies of every persuasion, especially windsurfing and hobie cat enthusiasts.

For those seeking quieter pleasures, the Robberg and Keurbooms River nature reserves are ideal getaways. The 175-hectare (432-acres) sandstone promontory that is the **Robberg Nature Reserve** juts about 4 kilometres (2.5 miles) into the sea. Much of this area has been declared a marine reserve, so permits are required (available at the entrance). The furthest point of the reserve is known as Cape Seal – the term 'robberg' means 'seal mountain' – because of the hundreds of seals that lived here when Khoi Strandlopers walked these shores. Robberg is a breeding ground for seabirds, including cormorants, gulls and oystercatchers. The **Keurbooms River Nature Reserve** to the northeast of the town adjoins both the Keurbooms River State Forest and the Whiskey Creek Nature Reserve, home of the Plettenberg Bay Angling Club. The atmosphere here is relaxed, with many activities for both young and old including fishing, watersports and bird-watching.

offered within the town and has been accused of detracting from the natural aesthetics of the area and jeopardising the local environment.

Leisure activities abound in the area, and range from bird-watching and hiking – there are many demarcated trails in the local forests, including the famous 100-kilometre (62-mile), eight-day **Outeniqua Hiking Trail** – to scenic drives and guided drives through local game farms. Because of the easy access to the lake and the sea, watersports are plentiful and include canoe trips, diving and cruises on the lagoon. Visitors may also hire houseboats, and the *John Benn* entertains guests as they cruise the quiet waters.

Accessible only via the Featherbed ferry or by private boat, the **Featherbed Nature Reserve** sprawls across the slopes of the western Head, at the entrance to the Knysna Lagoon. The 70-hectare (173-acre) reserve is geared largely toward conservation, with educational tours for schools and other special-interest groups concentrating on the ecology of the region. The terrain covered by the reserve also includes hiking trails, among them the 2.2-kilometre (1.2-mile), one-hour Bushbuck Trail, and a 5-kilometre (3-mile) trail along a more scenic and less strenuous route. All hikes through the reserve must be led by an approved guide.

Plettenberg Bay

The landscape around Tsitsikamma and Plettenberg Bay comprises several conservation areas – there are more plant varieties here than in the entire northern hemisphere – and marine reserves. At the same time, the area depends on seasonal visitors – so much is made of the blessings of nature, with plenty of horse-riding routes, waterways for canoeing and trails reserved for hikers. With its pristine beaches, sparkling waters and emerald forest backdrop,

Tsitsikamma

The fynbos and forests of the Outeniqua and Tsitsikamma are undoubtedly the Cape's most beautiful, and are exceptionally rich in wildlife – especially birds, which number over 280 different species. The area is blessed with a high rainfall and water is integral to the ecology of the region: the source of the Storms River is in the high wetlands and the landscape is laced with mountain streams.

The **Tsitsikamma section of the Garden Route National Park** stretches for approximately 80 kilometres (50 miles) along the coast and extends about 5 kilometres (3 miles) out into the Indian Ocean, enclosing a precious marine reserve that is home to dolphins, whales and an array of seashore life. Qualified scuba divers can follow underwater trails to view the sealife first hand, but the experience onshore is equally rewarding. The landscape, including the adjacent forest, with its giant Outeniqua yellowwoods, assegaai and other tree species, is home to indigenous flora such as orchids and lilies. The Tsitsikamma forest is also home to common mammals such as baboon, duiker and grysbok, and even the rare Cape clawless otter, after which the popular 50-kilometre (31-mile) **Otter Trail** is named. In addition to the Otter Trail, there are a number of other walks and hikes within the confines of the national park, which now encompasses former state forests and the De Vasselot area.

OPPOSITE TOP *Popular Plettenberg Bay is a favoured resort of fun-seekers and holidaymakers.*

OPPOSITE BOTTOM LEFT *The beautiful Knysna turaco (loerie) is an unofficial symbol of the Garden Route.*

OPPOSITE BOTTOM RIGHT *Over many aeons, ocean waves have helped carve formations such as Cathedral Rock at Keurbooms.*

ABOVE *Lined with age-old yellowwood trees, the Outeniqua Trail features high on the destination list of hikers.*

USEFUL INFORMATION

Cango Caves Museum: tel: 044 272-7410; www.cangocaves.co.za
Cango Ostrich Farm: tel: 044 272-4623; www.cangoostrich.co.za
Cango Wildlife Ranch: Baron van Reede St, Oudtshoorn; tel: 044 272-5593; www.cango.co.za
CP Nel Museum: 3 Baron van Reede St, Oudtshoorn; tel: 044 272-7306; www.cpnelmuseum.co.za
Featherbed Nature Reserve: tel: 044 381-0590 (office), tel: 044 382-1693 (bookings); www.featherbed.co.za
Gamka Nature Reserve: tel: 021 659-3500 (bookings)
Garden Route National Park: tel: 044 302 5606; www.sanparks.org/garden_route
Garden Route Trails: tel: 044 883-1015; www.gardenroutetrails.co.za
George Information Centre: 124 York St; tel: 044 801-9295; www.georgetourism.co.za
George Museum: Courtney St; tel: 044 873-5343; geo.museum@mweb.co.za
Goukamma Nature Reserve: tel: 044 383-0042 (enquiries), 021 659-3500 (bookings); www.capenature.org.za
Highgate Ostrich Show Farm: tel: 044 272-7115; www.highgate.co.za
Itulu Game Farm: tel: 044 876-0313
John Benn Pleasure Boat: tel: 044 382-1693; www.knysnafeatherbed.com;
Knysna Museum: Queen St; tel: 044 302-6320
Knysna Oyster Trail (Knysna Tourism Bureau): tel: 044 382-5510
Knysna Tourism Bureau: 40 Main St; open 8am–5pm Mon–Sat; tel: 044 382-5510; www.tourismknysna.co.za
Mossel Bay Tourism Bureau: cnr Market/Church Rd; open 8am–6pm Mon–Fri, 9am–4pm Sat–Sun; tel: 044 691-2202; www.visitmosselbay.co.za
Oudtshoorn Information Centre: Voortrekker Rd; open 8am–5pm Mon–Fri, 9am–5pm Sat–Sun; tel: 044 279-2532/3; www.oudtshoorn.co.za
Outeniqua Hiking Trail: tel: 044 302-5606
Plettenberg Bay Tourism: Open 9am–5pm Mon–Fri, 9am–2pm Sat, 9am–1pm Sun; tel: 044 533-4065; www.plettenbergbay.co.za
Safari Ostrich Show Farm: Open 8am–4pm daily; tel: 044 272-7311; safariostrich@mweb.co.za
Sedgefield Information Bureau: Open 8.30am–4.30pm Mon–Sat; tel: 044 343-2658/2007; www.tourismsedgefield.co.za
Spring Street Gallery: 19 Spring St, Knysna; tel: 044 382-2233
Tsitsikamma National Park: tel: 042 281-1607; www.sanparks.org
Wilderness National Park: tel: 044 877-1197; www.sanparks.org

After a trip along the Garden Route, travellers may choose to put their feet up at **Nature's Valley**, a charming village and reserve at the foot of the Groot River Pass. Virtually enclosed by the tall trees and lush woods of the Tsitsikamma forest and surrounding mountains, it is an ideal setting to catch your breath and unwind.

DIRECTORIES

Shopping • Cuisine • Nightlife • Events

Shopping

Cape Town is considered by many to be the shopping capital of South Africa, and the city has all sorts of shopping experiences to tempt you. Like much of South Africa, Capetonians are spending more and more time and money bargain-hunting at flea markets and roadside stalls in addition to shopping at the established department stores and retail outlets. The city's current explosion of development has meant higher and higher turnover for everything from shopping malls to designer boutiques and even grocery stores.

Naturally, many of the tourist attractions, from the most obscure to the most visited, have their own 'in-house' shops, selling curios, souvenirs, crafts and books.

The pavements of many business districts, such as the city centre and suburbs such as Claremont, Wynberg, Muizenberg, Hout Bay and others, are lined with open-air markets that stock an assortment of goods – usually at very reasonable prices. The items here tend to be mass-produced, but there are also stalls selling African crafts such as wire toys, soapstone busts, wooden statuettes, beadwork, basketware and woven goods. Although it is virtually impossible to tell whether these have been made by entrepreneurial locals or within the confines of a local 'factory' – in fact, many originate in Zimbabwe and other neighbouring countries – they are probably handmade, and do represent indigenous African handcrafts.

Antiques

Because it is the oldest European settlement in southern Africa, Cape Town tends to be the country's antique capital. Many of the genuine articles – and certainly the real bargains – may be found at small, out-of-the-way dealers who do not, in fact, cater for the antique market at all. Of course, with the influx of bargain-hunters and the realisation that there is a demand for old Cape furniture, Victorian jewellery and old china, prices are rising, and many dealers are cashing in. Nevertheless, shoppers are sure to find at least one piece worth buying.

Some of the most popular hunting grounds are what has become known as the '**Antique Market**' along the pavements of Church, Burg and Long streets in the city centre; the Main Road of Kalk Bay, especially **Kalk Bay Antiques Centre**, 76b Main Rd, Kalk Bay, tel: 021 788-8882, and **Kalk Bay Trading Post**, 71 Main Road, Kalk Bay, tel: 021 788-9571; and along Main Road, which winds through the southern suburbs, especially in Woodstock, Observatory and Mowbray through Wynberg, Diep River and beyond.

ABOVE *The bountiful farmlands outside the city furnish local vendors with plenty of tempting fresh produce.*

OPPOSITE *A modern office tower dwarfs a picturesque décor and lifestyle store at the corner of Long and Church streets.*

Antique dealers include **Julian Adler Antiques & Africana** (by appointment only), Loop St, tel: 021 465-1090; **Burr & Muir**, 82 Church St, Cape Town, tel: 021 422-1319; **Tim Curtis Antiques**, Constantia Courtyard, **Constantia Mann**, tel: 021 794-0249; **Hans Niehaus Collectors Specialist**, 37 Vineyard Road, Claremont, tel: 021 674-3901; **Randall Hare Antiques**, Constantia Road, Wynberg, tel: 021 762-9362; and **Le Brocanteur**, 67 Constantia Main Road, Constantia, tel: 021 761-9142.

Art

Much like elsewhere, quality contemporary art is expensive in Cape Town, and visitors are advised to buy through reputable art dealers, such as: **Alpha Fine Art**, 730 Anreith cnr, Hans Strijdom Ave, Cape Town, tel: 021 418-2320; **João Ferreira Gallery**, 70 Loop St, Cape Town, tel: 021 423-5403; **Michael Stevenson Gallery**, Buchanan Building, 160 Sir Lowry Rd, Woodstock, tel: 021 462-1500; **The Cape Gallery**, 60 Church St, Cape Town, tel: 021 423-5309; **Everard Read Gallery**, 3 Portswood Rd, V&A Waterfront, tel: 021 418-4527; and **Die Kunskamer**, 3 Portswood Rd, V&A Waterfront, tel: 021 419-3226.

There are a number of local outlets for talented artists who may not have the clout to exhibit in up-market galleries or be represented by the top art dealers. Most of the informal art-and-craft markets so prolific over summer weekends on the peninsula sell the works of budding artists and craftspeople, and so do the more popular outdoor markets such as **Greenmarket Square**, **St George's Mall**, **Kirstenbosch Craft Market**, the **Hout Bay Market**, **Art-in-the-Park** on Silwood Road in Rondebosch, and on the verge outside the **Constantia Nek Restaurant** in Constantia.

There are many smaller galleries dotted around the Cape – such as those along the **Kalk Bay Main Road** – that exhibit the works of local artists and craftspeople. One of the most exciting art ventures is **FATE** (Facilitators for Art and Travelling Exhibitions) based in Velddrif on the West Coast. Contact Juli Olivier, 190 Voortrekker Road, Velddrif, tel: 022 783-1575.

Important local collections may be seen at the **South African National Gallery**, Government Avenue, Gardens, tel: 021 467-4660; **Rust-en-Vreugd**, 78 Buitenkant St, Cape Town, tel: 021 464-3280; **Old Town House** – Michaelis Art Collection, Greenmarket Sq, Cape Town, tel: 021 481-3933; **Irma Stern Museum**, Cecil Rd, Rosebank, tel: 021 685-5686; **Sasol Art Museum**, tel: 021 808-3695; **University of Stellenbosch Art Gallery**, tel: 021 808-3489; and **Stellenbosch Art Gallery**, tel: 021 887-8343.

Books

Ask any Capetonian where to buy second-hand books and you'll be directed to Long Street in the city centre, home to some of the most famous bookstores in the country. Top of the list are **Clarke's Bookshop**, 211 Long St, Cape Town, tel: 021 423-5739; **Clarke's Africana & Rare Books**, 26 Belair Dr., Constantia, tel: 021 794-0600; and **Select Books**, 232 Long St, Cape Town, tel: 021 424-6955. Also worth a visit are **Cafda Bookshop**, Werdmuller Centre, Main Rd, Claremont, tel: 021 674-2230, and Mimosa Arcade, 18 Regent Rd, Sea Point, tel: 021 434-6149. Other book dealers include **The Caxton Bookshop**, Warrington Rd, Kenilworth, tel: 021 683-6654; **Book Lounge**, 71 Roeland St, Cape Town, tel: 021 462-2425; **Kalk Bay Books**, 124 Main Rd, Kalk Bay, 021 788-2266; **Help the Rural Child Charity Bookshop**, 6 Victoria St, Mowbray, tel: 021 689-8392; and **Tommy's Book Shop**, 130 Long St, Cape Town, tel: 021 424-8675.

The main bookselling chains are: **Exclusive Books**: Cape Town International Airport, Shop 6, Domestic Departures Lounge, tel: 021 934-5873; Canal Walk, tel: 021 555-3720; Cavendish Square, Claremont, tel: 021 674-3030; Constantia Village, Spaanschemat Rd, Constantia, tel: 021 794-7800; Somerset Mall, Somerset West, tel: 021 851-0248; Stellenbosch, 14 Andringa Street, Stellenbosch, tel: 021 886-9277; 225 Victoria Wharf, V&A Waterfront, tel: 021 419-0905; **CNA (Central News Agency)**: Customer Care Share Call 0860 692 274; **PNA**: Plumstead, tel: 021 762-3433; Cape Gate, Debron Road, tel: 021 981-0787; and **Wordsworth Books**: Gardens, tel: 021 461-8464; Longbeach Mall, Noordhoek, tel: 021 785-5311; Willowbridge Centre, Tyger Valley, tel: 021 914-1791; Victoria Wharf, V&A Waterfront, tel 021 425-6880. Naturally, the curio shops at all the top tourist spots, such as Table Mountain, Kirstenbosch National Botanical Garden and others, stock publications covering the destination itself and related topics.

Clothing

As a fashion design centre, the Cape Peninsula boasts many clothing outlets, ranging from the designer wear of exclusive boutiques to the casual wear – and more – from the many factory shops that abound in semi-industrial suburbs throughout the city. For a comprehensive list of these factory outlets – although all boast 'factory prices', not all keep their promise – consult Pam Black's *A-to-Z of Factory Shops*, published by the author herself and available at most bookshops. Magnificent vintage gems such as classic beaded gowns, fur jackets, crocheted shawls, embroidered bags and silk gloves can be found at **Secondhand Rose**, Cavendish Close, Warwick St, Claremont, tel: 021 674-4270; **Deja Vu**, 278 Main Rd, Kenilworth, tel: 021 797-7373; and **Second Time Around**, 196 Long St, Cape Town, tel: 021 423-1674. Both new and second-hand clothes may be bought at the local markets – Greenmarket Square, Constantia, Kirstenbosch, Cape Town Station and Hout Bay. If you're looking for fabric, don't miss the ocean of materials available on market days at the **Grand Parade** in Darling St, or visit **Mnandi**, 90 Station Rd, Observatory, tel: 021 447-6814.

Most of the informal markets sell mostly handcrafted garments, but if this is your taste, then make a point of visiting the small boutiques and craft outlets along Main Road in Hout Bay, especially **Africa Nova** in Hout Bay as well as in Waterkant St, De Waterkant, tel: 021 435-5123. You'll find handmade garments at both the **Blue Shed Waterfront Craft Market** and the **Red Shed** at the V&A Waterfront. Remember, too, that many of the small towns in the Western Cape, and particularly those that serve rural communities, boast many outlets selling homemade clothes, many of which are of very good quality – such as **Le Cott Gifts & Decor**, Paarl Mall, Paarl, tel: 021 863-4181.

If, however, you're more at home with the designer look, the city is not only home to many of the country's premier couturiers, but also to a wide selection of exclusive fashion salons. Many are concentrated in and around the plush shopping malls such as **Cavendish Square** in Claremont, the **Tyger Valley Centre** in Durbanville, the **Somerset Mall** in Somerset West, the **Canal Walk** shopping centre at Century City, the **Constantia Village** centre in Constantia and the **Victoria Wharf** at the V&A Waterfront.

At the same time, however, don't ignore the established chain stores as many represent some of the big fashion names of Europe and the US, including Calvin Klein, Diesel, Levi Strauss, and other sought-after brand names. A local favourite, **Young Designers Emporium**, Cavendish Square, Claremont, tel: 021 683-6177; Canal Walk, tel: 021 555-2090; Somerset Mall, tel: 021 852-0764; and V&A Waterfront, tel: 021 425-6232, is a co-operative venture providing an outlet for the talented new young designers on the fashion front.

While the high-fashion stores are lined wall-to-wall with designer names, there are less ostentatious outlets that stock casual attire and sportswear at reasonable prices – the **Woolworths** and **Edgars** chains of stores being firm favourites with locals.

To hire fancy dress, costumes and even evening wear, the best known dealer is **Sue Farmer Costumes**, 55 Morningside, Pinelands, tel: 021 531-5919; Bellville, 16 Voortrekker Rd,

Bellville, tel: 021 949-5782; and trading as **Fancy That** in Parklands, tel: 021 557-7012.

Crafts, Curios and Souvenirs

Cape Town is filled with crafts and curios representing the indigenous people of the subcontinent. Some are authentic, some are not; some are exquisite, and some of very poor quality; some are outrageously expensive, others remarkably cheap – and all may be found at up-market curio shops, middle-of-the-road souvenir outlets, and informal roadside stalls.

The peninsula's plethora of flea markets – at Constantia, Kirstenbosch and Hout Bay, for example – all sell indigenous crafts, as do the established markets at **Greenmarket Square**, **Muizenberg** and **Milnerton**. Informal roadside stalls, such as that outside the Tourism Gateway on Adderley St and along the fringe of Cape Town railway station, also sell curios.

Curios as well as customised souvenirs can be found at most of the city's popular tourist attractions, such as Kirstenbosch, Table Mountain, Groot Constantia, Cape Point, Mariner's Wharf in Hout Bay and, of course, the **Blue Shed Waterfront Craft Market**, tel: 021 408-7840, and the **Red Shed**, at the V&A Waterfront, V&A Visitors' Info Centre, tel: 021 408-7600; and the vibrant **Pan-African Market**, 76 Long St, Cape Town, tel: 021 426-4478. Other opportunities to buy local crafts, curios and souvenirs may be had at **African Art**, Witsands Rd, Scarborough, tel: 021 780-9904; **Indaba Curios**, 1 Pierhead, V&A Waterfront, tel: 021 425-3639; **Induna Gallery**, The Palms Centre, Sir Lowry Rd, Woodstock, tel 021 462-3374; and **Out of Africa**, 125 Victoria Wharf, V&A Waterfront, tel: 021 418-5505.

The smaller towns outside the peninsula also have Saturday-morning craft markets, and specialised curio outlets. These include **The Little Wool Shop**, Delvera Farm, R44, Stellenbosch, tel: 021 884 4004; **Worcester Museum Complex** on Robertson Rd, Worcester, tel: (023) 342-2225; and **Ikhwezi Community Centre**, Jan van Riebeeck Dr., Paarl, tel: 021 868-1707.

If you are looking for gems and traditional African jewellery, be sure to visit the markets and jewellers in most of the shopping malls, or any of the craft and curio outlets listed opposite, but

ABOVE *Cape Town's hawkers have brought the shopping experience from the malls to the streets.*

OPPOSITE *Taking pride of place among the city's many malls is the handsome Victoria Wharf at the V&A Waterfront.*

also visit **Afrogem**, 64 New Church St, Cape Town, tel: 021 424-8048.

Markets

Probably the most popular shopping venue in South Africa is the market: flea market, craft market, street market, fish market and produce market. Like much of the country, Cape Town has its fair share of informal stalls and kiosks lining the pavements of the city and suburbs, and filling virtually every possible stretch of open ground over weekends.

The most renowned of the city's informal market places is the **Grand Parade** on Darling Street and **Greenmarket Square**, an eclectic collection of second-hand goods, trendy fashion, collectibles and junk. Weekends see a mushrooming of similar markets: the bric-a-brac stalls of the **Muizenberg Flea Market** off Sunrise Circle, the arts and crafts of **Art-in-the-Park** in Rondebosch, **Kirstenbosch Craft Market**, and the handmade goods on **Hout Bay's Main Road**. For good organic produce, visit The Neighbourgoods Market at **The Old Biscuit Mill** in Woodstock and the **Porter Estate Produce Market** in Tokai.

The markets at the **V&A Waterfront**, however, are extremely popular, and visitors and locals alike flock there to sift through the goods of the **Red Shed** and the **Waterfront Craft Market** in the Blue Shed. Prices here tend to cater for tourists who benefit from the favourable exchange rate, so if you're looking for bargains, you may decide to visit the less lavish markets that have become commonplace in the city streets.

Neighbouring towns, moreover, also tend to offer much along the lines of casual weekend markets. Stellenbosch boasts the **Winelands Craft Market** (every Sunday during summer); Paarl has its own flea market (off Main St) and an **Art and Craft Market** (in Victoria Park on the first Saturday of the month), as do several towns in the vicinity, such as Worcester, Hermanus, Langebaan and others.

Shopping Malls

Considering its modest size in relation to the shopping meccas of Paris, New York, Rome, London, Singapore and even Johannesburg, Cape Town boasts an array of sophisticated department stores and an equally impressive number of shopping malls. All the larger business centres have at least one complex devoted to the shopping experience, generally anchored by one or more of the leading department or chain stores. Although some of the smaller neighbouring towns are somewhat limited in variety, Saturday mornings see malls buzzing with regular shoppers. The busiest, more popular shopping malls are **Cavendish Square**, Claremont, tel: 021 657-5600; **Victoria Wharf**, V&A Waterfront Info Centre, tel: 021 408-7600; **Lifestyles On Kloof**, 50 Kloof Street, Cape Town; **Riverside Shopping Centre**, Rondebosch, tel: 021 685-4442; **Constantia Village**, Constantia, tel: 021 794-5065; **Blue Route Mall**, Tokai, tel: 021 713-2360; **The Gardens Shopping Centre**, Gardens, tel: 021 465-1842; **The Alfred Mall**, V&A Waterfront, tel: 021 419-9507; **Cavendish Connect**, Claremont, tel: 021 657-5600; **Maynard Mall**, Wynberg, tel: 021 797-1714; **Kenilworth Centre**, Kenilworth, tel: 021 671-5054; **Longbeach Mall**, Noordhoek, tel: 021 785-5955; **Tyger Valley Centre**, tel: 021 914-1822; **Somerset Mall**, tel: 021 852-7114/5; **Northgate Island**, Paarden Island, tel: 021 511-4808; and **Canal Walk**, Century City, tel: 021 555-4444. There are more intimate shopping centres, which house the country's most popular stores.

Cuisine

Traditional Fare

For the best traditional Cape fare in the finest settings, visitors should consider the up-market eateries of Constantia. Rated among the country's finest restaurants are **Buitenverwachting**, Klein Constantia Rd, Constantia, tel: 021 794-3522, and **Constantia Uitsig**, Spaanschemat River Rd, Constantia, tel: 021 794-4480.

Restaurants with an African theme include **Africa Café**, 108 Shortmarket St, Cape Town, tel: 021 422-0221; **De Volkskombuis**, Aan de Wagenweg, Stellenbosch, tel: 021 887-2121; **Emily's**, top floor, Clock Tower Centre, V&A Waterfront, tel: 021 421-1133; and **Mama Africa**, 178 Long St, Cape Town, tel: 021 424-8634. There are also some notable

restaurants on popular wine estates. **Moyo**, Spier Wine Estate, info@spier.co.za, www.spier.co.za, tel: 021 809-1133, on the Stellenbosch Wine Route, offers a unique dining experience in the tradition of Africa – a sumptuous outdoor buffet served in a tree-lined garden dotted with Bedouin tents. Also highly regarded are **Boschendal**, Pniel Rd, Groot Drakenstein, tel: 021 874-1252, and **The Governor's Hall** at the Lanzerac, Stellenbosch, tel: 021 887-1132.

Fast Foods

Eat-on-the-run meals are easy to come by in Cape Town. **Victoria Wharf** and the **King's Warehouse** on the V&A Waterfront have plenty of takeaway joints, and vendors sell their wares (often *samoosas* and other traditional finger foods) at the Grand Parade and at many corner shops throughout the city. Similar outlets are also found at the more popular beaches and in shopping malls. Watch for **McDonald's**, **KFC**, **Nando's Chicken**, **Steers**, **Marcel's Frozen Yoghurt**, **St Elmo's Pizzaway** and **Kauai** for a healthier option.

Seafood

For the best fish and seafood, try the following: **Black Marlin**, Main Rd, Miller's Point, tel: 021 786-1621; **Blue Peter Hotel's Upper Deck**, Popham Rd, Bloubergstrand, tel: 021 554-1956; **Brass Bell**, Main Rd, Kalk Bay, tel: 021 788-5455; **Burgundy**, Market Square, Harbour Rd, Hermanus, tel: 028 312-2800; **Panama Jack's**, Quay 500, Cape Town Harbour, tel: 021 447-3992; **Die Strandloper**, Beach Rd, Langebaan, tel: 022 772-2490; **Mariner's Wharf**, Hout Bay Harbour, tel: 021 790-1100; and **The Cape Town Fish Market**: Camps Bay, tel: 021 438-1866; Canal Walk, tel: 021 555-1950; GrandWest, tel: 021 535-3110; Tyger Valley, tel: 021 914-9151; V&A Waterfront, tel: 021 418-5977.

Cafés and Bistros

Cape Town has its fair share of both up-market and casual bistros: **San Marco**, Victoria Wharf, V&A Waterfront, tel: 021 418-5434; **Obz Café**, 115 Lower Main Rd, Observatory, tel: 021 448-5555; **News Café**, Artscape Theatre Centre, DF Malan St, Cape Town, tel: 021 421-1425; **Mano's**, 39 Main Rd, Green Point, tel: 021 434-1090; **Robert's Café**, 72 Waterkant St, De Waterkant, tel: 021 425-7669; and **Summerville**, Victoria Rd, Camps Bay, tel: 021 438-9551.

Popular Eateries

Many of the trendiest restaurants have unique attractions. Some are fashionable, while others simply offer fine food in an exquisite setting. Reservations are essential at the following: **Gardener's Cottage**, Montebello Estate, 31 Newlands Ave, Newlands, tel: 021 689-3158; **Jake's on Summerley**, 5 Summerley Rd, Kenilworth, tel: 021 797-0366; **Jake's in the Village**, Steenberg Village, Steenberg Rd, Constantia, tel: 021 701-3272; **Simon's**, Groot Constantia, tel: 021 794-1143; **221**, Victoria Wharf, V&A Waterfront, tel: 021 418-3633; **Balducci's**, Victoria Wharf, V&A Waterfront, tel: 021 421-6002; **Myoga at The Vineyard**, Colinton Rd, Newlands, tel: 021 657-4545; **Two Oceans**, Cape Point, tel: 021 780-9200, 021 702-0703 (bookings); **Blues**, Promenade, Victoria Rd, Camps Bay, tel: 021 438-2040; **Cantina Tequila**, Belville, tel: 021 919-1556; **The Wild Fig**, Valkenberg Estate, Liesbeek Parkway, Mowbray, tel: 021 448-0507; and **Suikerbossie**, Victoria Drive, Hout Bay, tel: 021 790-1450.

For Oriental or Indian cuisine, an absolute must is the award-winning **Beijings Chinese Restaurant**, 26 Oxford St, Durbanville, tel: 021 975-1024. Also try **Mr Chan**, 178A Main Rd, Sea Point, tel: 021 439-2239, and **Chef Pon's Asian Kitchen**, Mill St, Gardens, tel: 021 465-5846. For Indian cuisine try **Perima's**, Belvedere Rd, Claremont, tel: 021 671-3205, and **Chandani Restaurant**, 85 Roodebloem Rd, Woodstock, tel: 021 447-7887.

Top Restaurants

A number of restaurants combine exceptional cuisine, fine service and a magnificent setting. The best of the best include **Cape Colony**, Mount Nelson Hotel, 76 Orange St, Gardens, tel: 021 483-1948; **La Maison de Chamonix**, Chamonix Estate, Uitkyk St, Franschhoek, tel: 021 876-2393; **Bosman's**, Grande Roche Hotel, cnr Plantasie/Constantia rds, Paarl, tel: 021 863-2727; **The Tasting Room at Le Quartier Français**, 16 Huguenot St, Franschhoek, tel: 021 876-2151; **La Petite Ferme**, Pass Rd, Franschhoek, tel: 021 876-3016; **Savoy Cabbage**, 101 Hout St, Cape Town, tel: 021 424-2626; **Ginja**, 121 Castle

St, Cape Town, tel: 021 426-2368; **Pigalle**, 57 Somerset Rd, Green Point, tel: 021 421-4848; and **Belthazar Wine Bar and Grill**, Victoria Wharf, V&A Waterfront, tel: 021 421-3753.

Mediterranean

Many local menus concentrate on the rich, filling food of the Mediterranean: **Café Paradiso**, 110 Kloof St, Gardens, tel: 021 423-8653; **Dias Tavern** (Portuguese), 15 Caledon St, Cape Town, tel: 021 465-7547; **La Perla** (Italian), cnr Church and Beach rds, Sea Point, tel: 021 434-2471; **Anatoli** (Turkish), 24 Napier St, Cape Town, tel: 021 419-2501; **Signal**, Cape Grace Hotel, West Quay, V&A Waterfront, tel: 021 418-0520; **Mnandi's**, Solole Game Reserve, Noordhoek, tel: 021 785-3248; **La Cantina**, The Palms, Sir Lowry Rd, Cape Town, tel: 021 462-7428; **Greek**, 78 Durban Rd, Mowbray, tel: 021 686-4314; **Marc's Mediterranean Cuisine**, 129 Main St, Paarl, tel: 021 863-3980; and **Thirty7**, Westin Grand, Cape Town, tel: 021 412-9999.

Out of the Ordinary

Top among dining alternatives are: **New York Bagels**, corner Regent/Clarens rds, Sea Point, tel: 021 439-7523, a fine deli outlet with a focus on bagels made famous in the Big Apple; **The Sea Horse**, Pierhead, V&A Waterfront, tel: 021 419-3122, a floating restaurant berthed at the V&A Waterfront; and, overlooking Table Bay, **Top of the Ritz**, Ritz Hotel, Rhine Rd, Sea Point, tel: 021 439-6983, the city's only revolving restaurant. Enjoy fine dining as well as the screening of a classic movie at **Azure** at The Twelve Apostles, Victoria Rd, Camps Bay, tel: 021 437-9029.

Fresh Food and Delicatessens

For the finest fresh fish and sushi, try the **Cape Town Fish Market**, King's Warehouse, V&A Waterfront, tel: 021 418-5977; **Willoughby & Co**, Victoria Wharf, V&A Waterfront, tel: 021 418-6116; Kalk Bay's **Harbour House**, tel: 021 788-4133; and Hout Bay's **Mariner's Wharf**, tel: 021 790-1100 for fish and seafood.

The Cape's finest delis include: **Giovanni's**, Main Rd, Green Point, tel: 021 434-6893; **Oakhurst Deli Shoppe**, Main Rd, Kenilworth, tel: 021 762-1539; **Noordhoek Village Farmstall**, 1 Village Lane, Noordhoek, tel: 021 789-1317; **Olympia Café and Deli**, 134 Main Rd, Kalk Bay, tel: 021 788-6396; **The Barnyard Farmstall**, Steenberg Rd, Tokai tel: 021 712-6934; **Melissa's – The Food Shop:** Gardens,

tel: 021 424-5540; Victoria Wharf, V&A Waterfront, tel: 021 418-0255; Newlands, tel: 021 683-6949; Constantia, tel: 021 794-4696; Tyger Valley, tel: 021 914-7608; and **Newport Market & Deli**, 47 Beach Rd, Mouille Point, tel: 021 439-1538.

Wine

As the heart of the country's wine industry, the Cape and its winelands offer an almost unlimited number of outlets for fine wines. Apart from the estates of Stellenbosch, Paarl, Franschhoek and even Constantia, try city stockists such as **Vaughan Johnson's Wine Shop**, Market Square, V&A Waterfront, tel: 021 419-2121; **Steven Rom Exporters**, Sea Point, tel: 021 439-6043; the **Olde Wine Shoppe**, Mariner's Wharf, Hout Bay, tel: 021 790-1100; **The Wine Shop at Constantia Uitsig**, Spaanschemat River Rd, Constantia, tel: 021 794-1810; **Manuka Café and Fine Wines**, Steenberg Village, Reddam Avenue, tel: 021 701-9777; Somerset West, cnr Main/Dummer rds, tel: 021 851-6060; **Shop 9, Manuka Wine Boutique**, Noordhoek Farm Village, tel: 021 789-0898; **Chenin Restaurant and Wine Bar**, Waterkant St, De Waterkant, tel: 021 425-2200; **Caveau Wine Bar and Deli**, 92 Bree St, Cape Town, tel: 021 422-1367; **Caroline's Fine Wine Cellar**, Strand St, Cape Town, tel: 021 419-8984; and on the Garden Route, **34° South**, Knysna Quays, tel: 044 382-7331.

Nightlife

Nightclubs, Pubs, Bars and Taverns

Whether it's after a long day at the office or a hot day on the beach, Capetonians flock to the city's many pubs and bars – and end up staying until the wee hours, especially if it's Friday. Some of the most popular city venues are **The Set**, Victoria Junction Hotel, Green Point, tel: 021 418-1234; **Salt**, Ambassador Hotel on the Rocks, Victoria Drive, Bantry Bay, tel: 021 439-6170; **Quay Four Tavern**, Quay 4, V&A Waterfront, tel: 021 419-2008; **Peddlar's on the Bend**, Spaanschemat River Rd, Constantia, tel: 021 794-7747; **Ferryman's**, East Pier Rd, V&A

Waterfront, tel: 021 419-7748; **Baraza Groove Bar**, Victoria Rd, Camps Bay, tel: 021 438-1758; and **The River Club**, Observatory, tel: 021 448-7357.

In contrast, Cape Town's club life, although lively is rather erratic. There are, however, favourite haunts that attract a loyal clientele. Among them are **Hemisphere, Mercury Live, Zula Sound Bar** and **The Assembly**. Watch the daily press for the launch of new clubs and one-off party extravaganzas, which tend to be very popular over the festive season. For Cape Town's 'party of the year', look out for details of the **Mother City Queer Project** (MCQP) annual extravaganza in December.

Theatre
Cape Town's theatres present a variety of dramatic, comic, dance and musical productions. The main theatre venues are **The Baxter Theatre Centre**, Main Rd, Rosebank, tel: 021 685-7880; **Artscape Theatre Centre**, DF Malan St, Cape Town, tel: 021 410-9800; **Theatre on the Bay**, Links St, Camps Bay, tel: 021 438-3301; **Maynardville Open-Air Theatre** (open January to February only), cnr Church/Wolfe streets, Wynberg, tel: 021 421-7839. Smaller but equally popular are **The Fugard Theatre**, cnr Caledon/Harrington streets, District 6, Cape Town, tel: 021 461-4554, www.thefugard.com; **The New Space Theatre**, 44 Long St, Cape Town, tel: 021 422-5522, www.newspacetheatre.co.za; and **The Intimate Theatre**, 37 Orange St, Gardens, Cape Town, tel: 021 480-7129, www.intimatetheatre.net. There are also a few community theatres dotted around the suburbs. These are usually small and intimate, but with innovative entertainment programmes. Book through **Computicket**, tel: 083 915 8000.

Music
All the city's theatres host music recitals ranging from classical to popular and, occasionally, traditional music. Watch the daily press for details of what is showing at **City Hall** on Darling Street, Cape Town; **V&A Waterfront Amphitheatre** at the V&A Waterfront; **Kirstenbosch Summer Concerts**; and both the **Oude Libertas Amphitheatre** and **Spier Open-Air Amphitheatre**, in Stellenbosch. Booking for most musical recitals can be done through Computicket.

For fine jazz, try the **Green Dolphin Restaurant**, Alfred Mall, V&A Waterfront, tel: 021 421-7471; **Marimba**, Cape Town International Convention Centre, tel: 021 418-3366; **Bascule Bar**, Cape Grace Hotel, V&A Waterfront, tel: 021 410-7100; **Hanover Street**, GrandWest Casino, Goodwood, tel: 021 505-7777; and **Dizzy's Jazz Café**, Camps Bay Drive, Camps Bay, tel: 021 438-2686.

The Buena Vista Social Café, 81 Main Rd, Green Point, tel: 021 433-0611, offers sultry, latin rhythms while the **Barleycorn Music Club**, Rygersdal Sports Club, Rondebosch, showcases the best of local talent in contemporary folk and pop-rock. For more information, visit the website www.barleycorn.org.za.

Cinema
All the major shopping malls have at least three or four cinemas showing the latest Hollywood releases and, occasionally, acclaimed foreign films (especially at Cinema Nouveau complexes at the V&A Waterfront and Cavendish Square malls). The major cinema chains are Ster-Kinekor and Nu-Metro, and the biggest venues are the **Blue Route Mall**, Retreat; **Maynard Mall**, Wynberg; **Kenilworth Centre**, Kenilworth; **Cavendish Square**, Claremont; **Victoria Wharf**, V&A Waterfront; **Tyger Valley Shopping Centre**, Tyger Valley, and **Canal Walk**, Century City; and **Longbeach Mall**, Noordhoek. The intimate **Labia Theatre**, 68 Orange St, Gardens, and the **Labia on Kloof**, 50 Kloof St, Gardens, tel: 021 424-5927, support independent films and attract a more critical movie-goer.

Book for all movies through Computicket or directly through Nu-Metro Cinemas, 086 110 0220 (bookings and enquiries) or Ster-Kinekor Cinemas, 086 130 0444 (bookings and enquiries).

Gambling
There are only two full-fledged casinos within reach of the city: **GrandWest Casino**, Vanguard Dr, Goodwood, tel: 021 505-7777, and **Caledon Hotel, Spa & Casino**, Caledon, tel: 028 214-5100. Gambling in South Africa is for people 18 years and older. The National Responsible Gambling counselling line is 0800 006 008 toll-free.

Cabaret
Cabaret venues are few in Cape Town, with most of the limited performances moving from small, intimate restaurants to established theatres. Establishments that concentrate on traditional cabarets include **The Kalk Bay Theatre**, Kalk Bay, tel: 073 220-5430; **On Broadway**, 88 Shortmarket St, Cape Town, tel: 021 424-1194; **The Roxy Revue Bar**, GrandWest Casino, Goodwood, tel: 021 505-7777; and **The NewSpace Theatre**, 44 Long St, Cape Town, tel: 021 422-5522. Be sure to watch the daily press for current news on these events.

Safety
As in all big cities, the night brings the need for vigilance. Cars parked in the centre of town may be at particular risk, so always lock your car, and never leave valuables inside. Park in a well-lit area or in a pay-as-you-park facility, and never walk alone to your car after dark. In an emergency, call the **Flying Squad** on 10111 for police assistance, and report any serious incident, such as a mugging, car accident or assault as soon as possible.

OPPOSITE *As they near the finish line of the gruelling* Cape Argus-Pick n Pay Cycle Tour, *held each year in March, cyclists pass palm-fringed Camps Bay Beach.*

Festivals and events in and around Cape Town

JANUARY
- Cape Minstrel Carnival (Cape Town)

FEBRUARY
- Shakespeare at Maynardville (Maynardville Open-Air Theatre, Wynberg)
- Design Indaba (CTICC, Cape Town)
- The Women's Show (CTICC, Cape Town)
- Opening of Parliament (CBD)
- J&B Metropolitan Handicap (Kenilworth Race Course)
- Infecting the City – The Spier Public Arts Festival (Cape Town)
- Community Chest Carnival (Maynardville, Wynberg)

MARCH
- Dragon Boat Festival (V&A Waterfront)
- Cape Argus Pick n Pay Cycle Tour (Cape Town)
- Klein Karoo National Arts Festival (Oudtshoorn)
- Navy Festival Regatta (Simon's Town)
- Cape Town Festival (CBD)

APRIL
- Decorex (CTICC, Cape Town)
- Cape Town International Jazz Festival (CTICC, Cape Town)
- Two Oceans Marathon (Cape Town)
- Cederberg Arts Festival (Clanwilliam)

MAY
- V&A Waterfront Wine Affair (V&A Waterfront)
- Good Food and Wine Show (CTICC)
- Cape Gourmet Festival (Cape Town)
- Franschhoek Literary Festival (Franschhoek)

JUNE
- Cape Town International Book Fair (CTICC, Cape Town)
- Snoek Derby, Hout Bay

JULY
- Funny Festival (Baxter Theatre, Rondebosch)
- Bastille Festival (Franschhoek)
- Knysna Oyster Festival (Knysna)
- Stellenbosch Wine Festival (Stellenbosch)

AUGUST
- Cape Town Fashion Week (CTICC, Cape Town)
- Clanwilliam Wildflower Show

SEPTEMBER
- Cape Town International Comedy Festival (Baxter Theatre, Rondebosch)
- Whale Festival (Hermanus)
- Nederburg Wine Auction (Stellenbosch)
- Darling Wild Flower Show (Darling)
- Persia to Paarl Wine Festival (Paarl)
- Cultivaria Festival (Paarl)
- Knysna Gastronomica (Knysna)
- Baxter Dance Festival (Baxter Theatre, Rondebosch)
- Spring Splash Annual Swim (Fish Hoek)

OCTOBER
- iTownship Wine Festival (Cape Town)
- Cape Town International Kite Festival (Zandvlei, Muizenberg)
- Annual Gun Run (Green Point)
- Cape Town Flower & Garden Show (Lourensford, Stellenbosch)
- Franschhoek Uncorked Festival (Franschhoek)
- Rocking the Daisies Music Festival (Darling)
- Khayelitsha Festival (Khayelitsha)

NOVEMBER
- Walk of Art Festival (De Waal Park, CBD)
- Cape Times Big Walk (CBD)

DECEMBER
- OBZ Festival (Observatory)
- Hout Bay Harbour Festival (Hout Bay)
- Mother City Queer Project (MCQP) Annual Party

INDEX

Page numbers in bold refer to photographs

Index

175